BRECON
168
MERTHYR
TYDVYL
Llangammarch
Crickadarn
Gwenddwr
Llandevalley
Llanstephan
Boughrood
Glasbury
Llanygan
Talgarth
HAY
Clyro
Llan Dewi Vach
Llanbedyr
Pains Castle
or Penquastle
Aber Edwy
Llangoed
and Castle
Pipton Chapel
Llan Elian
Trallong
Devenog
St. Davids
Llangynider
Ystradvelte
Penderyn
Vaenor
Dowlais
Iron Works
Bedwelty
Gelli Gaer
Llanvabon
New Bridge
Llysdinam
Llanleonvel
Capely Fyn
Llangattock

SWEET BEULAH LAND

SWEET BEULAH LAND
An intriguing insight into Welsh life between 1945 and 1951

by

ELWYN BOWEN

FOXGATE PRESS
MERTHYR TYDFIL

I've reached the land of corn and wine,
And all its riches freely mine;
Here shines undimmed one blissful day,
For all my night has passed away.

O Beulah Land, sweet Beulah Land,
As on thy highest mount I stand,
I look away across the sea,
Where mansions are prepared for me,
And view the shining glory shore:
My heaven, my home for evermore!

Reproduced from *Sacred Songs & Solos*
Harper CollinsReligious

Foxgate Press Publishers
Nantsiarad, Upper High Street
Cefn Coed y Cymer
Merthyr Tydfil CF48 2PH

Published by Foxgate Press Publishers 1999

ISBN 0 9513706 3 4

Copyright © Elwyn Bowen 1999

Printed and bound in Wales by
Stephens & George Ltd., Merthyr Tydfil

All rights reserved. No part of the publication may be reproduced, stored in a retrieval system, or transmitted, in any form or by any means, electronic, mechanical, photocopying, recording or otherwise, without the prior permission of the publishers.

Drawings by Dewi Bowen.

Publisher's Note

The old maps reproduced on the book end papers curiously do not show Beulah nor Cefn Coed y Cymer, which is a little curious when one considers the longevity of settlement in those areas. For the reader's information, Cefn Coed is just north of Merthyr Tydfil and Beulah lies between Llangammarch and Builth.

Contents

Introduction	13
My Early Year	17
Off to Beulah	27
The New School	37
The Food Inspector	59
A Community in Change	71
Poets, Dogs and Shepherds	81
Kicking Out the Squire	93
The Gamekeeper and a Woodland Encounter	105
Primitive but Necessary	113
Rural Poverty and Some Good Advice	133
The Eisteddfod and the Hunt Ball	145
Toilet Smashing and the 1947 Snow	161
To Everything there is a Season	175
Scotland Yard and Rural Characters	183

Foreword

THE STORY OF MOST Welsh people in the two hundred years down to 1950 was of industrialization, urbanization and migration from the countryside. This was certainly the history of Elwyn Bowen's family which, from the middle of the 19th century was working in the Dowlais Iron works or keeping the Morning Sun Inn built by his grandmother's father in 1851. And even before that the publican's father was Dafydd Lewis, Unitarian and a leader in the Merthyr Rising of 1831. Quite a pedigree, one which the young Elwyn maintained through childhood and schooling in 1930s Merthyr where his lifelong radicalism and humanism were well honed before war service and an eventual career after the war as a teacher and headmaster back on his own patch. But here's the rub, and the theme of this wonderfully evocative book - from 1945 - 1951 his personal life reversed the whole thrust of modern Welsh history and took him rather unexpectedly, to be headmaster of Llwyn Madoc School in Beulah near Builth. It was, in distance, almost a near neighbour of Merthyr Tydfil and it was, in culture, a world away.

Elwyn Bowen discovered a community in which traditional rural crafts and village self-sufficiency, all wrapped up in a society made and directed by a Welsh-language culture and its religious manifestation, still, but only just thrived. By the time he left it the economy of consumer goods, mass produced and shop bought, had already taken over. He was the witness to its last gasp. His scholarly work would later describe and analyze, in marvellous detail, how the rural and the urban here intertwined until one strangled the deep identity of the other. Now, in Sweet Beulah Land, though still steeped in that knowledge, he brushes in the colour of personality and the vivacity of anecdote to give us a book that is a delight to read for its capacity to breathe life back into that lost world.

Dr. Bowen's prose is as sparkling and enticing as the rivers his poachers fished in and as warm and compassionate as the men and women he portrays so brilliantly. Two Waleses met in those years and through the person of Elwyn Bowen. We have reason to be grateful it was so.

Professor Dai Smith
Head of Broadcast English Language
BBC Wales

Introduction

THESE STORIES REFLECT THE contrast between urban and rural life immediately after the Second World War and, perhaps more importantly, show the transition from self-sufficiency in the Welsh countryside to one of dependency upon external agencies. This theme later became my Ph.D. thesis, which was concerned with 'Traditional Industries of Breconshire' and the demise of rural craftsmen and of self-sufficiency.

I was brought up in Cefn Coed, an industrial village which served as a dormitory for the ironworkers and miners of nearby Merthyr Tydfil. At the age of twenty-one, after a brief period teaching at my old school, Vaynor and Penderyn Grammar School, I became Headmaster of Llwyn Madoc School, Beulah. This village of under thirty houses and a population of around one hundred residents, had a Post Office, two shops, a shoemaker, carpenter, wheelwright, nurse, blacksmith, church, chapel, vicarage, inn, a closed woollen factory and corn mill, a school of thirty-eight pupils and a school house. The village and the surrounding farms belonged to the Llwyn Madoc estate owned by the squire, Commander Evan Thomas, whose family had lived here for centuries.

Beulah is situated fourteen miles west of Builth in the Irfon Valley, north of the Epynt mountain range of north Breconshire. The spa town of Llanwrtyd is four miles further west and associated historically with the famous William Williams of Pantycelyn (1717-91), who was a curate here and at nearby Abergwesyn in 1740. The famous spa well at Llanwrtyd was discovered by the Reverend Theophilus Evans, Vicar of Llangamarch, author of *Drych y Prif Oesoedd* and grandfather of Theophilus Jones the county historian of Breconshire. At Llangamarch, two miles to the south-west, was Cefnbrith, the home of the famous Puritan martyr, John Penry (1563-93). Some ten miles along the road to Builth was Cilmeri, where Llewelyn ap Gruffudd, "Llewelyn Ein Llyw Olaf" – was killed on 11 December 1282.

This virtually self-sufficient society had remained almost unchanged for centuries. Its members understood their various roles as farmers, craftsmen, servants and labourers, males and females in an agrarian society and economy. They were bound by ties of kinship and marriage, as members of 'extended families', as members of neighbourhood and family work groups, co-operating together at times of high seasonal activity such as shearing or harvesting, or in lending or sharing horses or implements. In addition, there were strong ties of language, tradition and custom.

Although scattered, this rural society provided opportunities for shared religious, cultural and social activities through the church, chapel, the Beulah Eisteddfod, the Beulah Show and the all-important realization that 'mutual aid' and co-operation were necessary for economic survival. In addition, there were eisteddfodau at Llanwrtyd and Llangamarch, singing festivals in the chapels, and village dances and whist-drives at Christmas, Sunday School tea-parties and visits to the fairs and marts held at Builth. The seasonality of agricultural activity was reflected in the social life of the agricultural community. Leisure and ready money marked out May, October and November as relative holiday periods with the Eisteddfod and Show held in the Summer months.

Because, until recently, communities such as Beulah were largely self-sufficient, rarely was it necessary for the countryman or woman to leave their localities for the necessities of life. Most country-dwellers, in contrast to many urban people, lived and died in intimate co-existence, realizing all their ambitions within their own communities, to which they were bound by ties of kinship and neighbourliness, in a social and economic unity. Until this century, all the food needed by the community was grown locally, and from their animals they had meat, skins, wool and milk. From their gardens they had vegetables and fruit, while their pigs provided bacon, pork and lard. The local craftsmen made furniture, tools and implements, wove cloth, ground cereals for flour and meal; tanners made leather used by local bootmakers, saddlers made horse harness while the wheelwrights made wheels and gambos or carts.

There were significant changes in the local economy by the time I arrived at Beulah in the Spring of 1945. The Dolfelin corn mill and the Dolaeron woollen mill had closed, horse-drawn carts were being replaced by tractors and trailers, so that Dai Arthur the wheelwright and Jim Mathias were no longer making as many carts or wheels, nor shoeing as many horses as pre-war because of the growing popularity of cars, tractors and lorries. Bill Jones the shoemaker was no longer making many boots and shoes, but was reduced to repairing shoes bought at Builth. By the mid-1950s these three craft workshops were closed. I was fortunate to have seen these craftsmen working assiduously in their workshops, to have witnessed their great skills in transforming seasoned timber into oak furniture, gambos with a forty-year guarantee, wheels of elm, oak and ash for their different parts and implements, that would last a lifetime.

Many articles were made on the hearth on winter nights. The men would fashion walking sticks, shepherds' crooks, shafts for implements, rakes; Gib Lewis made his baskets while women made rag-mats, sewed, knitted and crocheted shawls and blankets. Today, hardly anything is made locally and commercially: most country people turn to the local towns to satisfy their needs in terms of food, clothes, cars or television sets or repairs.

Since 1945, because of mechanization and the reduction in labour on farms, the closure of the craft workshops, and the technological, economic and social changes, the depopulation of the countryside has resulted in the loss of natural leaders. All these factors have completely changed the life and outlook of the community. The closure of rural schools has deprived Beulah of a focus for parents and children, which for over a century had been an essential element in the fabric of a local culture.

This rural society had its own particular culture, built up by generations of people attending the same school, chapel and church, co-operating in the harvest fields or shearing and competing in the singing festivals and eisteddfodau. They transmitted it to the next generation by the socialization of their children, and through the corpus of customs, ideas, knowledge within certain patterns of living, and acceptable standards of behaviour broadly described as 'the Welsh way of life'.

As a result of these changes, Beulah and the Welsh countryside has lost more than individual units, schools, the eisteddfod or the many little Nonconformist chapels. It has also lost a particular local culture, embracing all these institutions and the native Welsh-speaking, colourful characters who wove this cultural fabric in the ordinary affairs of their daily lives.

The following brief stories reflect various incidents that touch upon this local culture of eisteddfodau, hunt balls, the Black Market, and rural poverty, during the period from 1945 to 1951. I hope they indicate too the arduous lives followed by country people in rural Wales striving to live in a sometimes harsh climate, and working a grudging soil. I trust that the sociological information included in the stories will be seen as necessary in providing a picture of a rural community in the final stages of change from self-sufficiency to one of dependency upon external agencies.

My Early Years

MY CLOSEST FRIEND CLAIMED that if I had fallen into a river of mud, I would have come out with a new suit on. He inferred by this that my life was blessed and he was correct. I was born in 1923, the son of the local nurse who had served as a nursing sister in the two World Wars, and a former soldier who had endured terrible hardships on the Dardanelles and Mesopotamia in the First World War, and was later employed at the Dowlais Iron Works where my grandmother's brother, Emmanuel Lewis, was the manager. My grandmother was the licensee of the Morning Sun Inn, Cefn Coed, built by her father in 1851; he was the son of Dafydd Lewis, Unitarian leader of the Merthyr Riots of 1831. The Inn was the rendezvous of ironworkers, miners, colliers, farmers, drovers and the local intelligentsia. Next door to the Inn lived my early mentor, the poet-historian, Tom Lewis (Mab-y-Mynydd), Alderman and Chairman of the local magistrates. Opposite lived another aunt and uncle and their six sons. This home exuded warmth, love and kindness, and the home of John and Ann Lewis was one of my favourite haunts as a child.

I grew up breathing, playing and living within my extended family of aunts, uncles and cousins. I was totally immersed socially and emotionally with dozens of cousins in tickling for fish, in swimming in Pwll Taf or Pwll Dan-y-Fynwent, raiding gardens, including our own, for gooseberries and searching for nuts or blackberries. We sold horse-mushrooms to a pregnant woman and nearly killed her, rode untamed horses, delivered lambs, kicked doors, sang carols in September, rode bicycles to Cardiff and Brecon, got knocked down and caught pneumonia by walking over the mountain to school to avoid an angry spinster. I had helped a News of the World photographer get a picture of her for five shillings. When her photograph appeared with the heading, 'Spinster sues aged farmer, alleged frequent kisses', I was put on her death-list. She daily searched for me like a falcon hunting its prey, so that the mountain mists and pneumonia was the only alternative option.

My closest friends were my younger brother, Dewi, my cousin Vivian who lived with his parents at the Morning Sun, and my cousins Trevor and Hugh who lived opposite. Hugh was a font of knowledge; he was an expert at finding birds' nests. The kingfisher's nest, or that of the peregrine falcon or golden hammer, were all the same to him. Even finding a cuckoo's egg presented no difficulty whatsoever. Whereas my uncle, Tom Lewis, spoke of Keats, Shelley and Wordsworth, Hugh was my mentor in all things related to natural life and music. He sang Richard Tauber's songs with an enchanting tenor voice and bewitched and teased the girls with his blue eyes, keen wit and handsome face.

He hated and rebelled against the Grammar School regime under the authoritarian headmaster, Trevor Lovett. He very frequently absented himself from school and spent his stolen days on the Darren Fawr, two miles north of Cefn Coed where his ancestor, Dafydd Lewis, had turned the 93rd Highland Regiment back to Brecon in the 1831 riots. Here in the remote windswept theatre of the moorland, he watched buzzards and falcons soaring and gliding. It was here that he was buried in a Neolithic cairn in 1973 after a brilliant career as a lecturer at Canterbury where his son became a chorister at the Cathedral.

Miraculously, I passed the eleven-plus entrance examination to the Vaynor and Penderyn Grammar School in 1935. This was at a time when we were temporarily living in the Morning Sun while my father was rebuilding our house. The Summer of 1935 was gloriously fine and warm, and the whole of August, from ten in the morning to ten at night was spent in Pwll-Dan-y-Fynwent (The pool under the cemetery). We came up briefly for dinner but cooked potatoes in the fire for tea. It was invariably pitch-dark when we made our way through the gravestones. Each day was filled with sunshine, fun and laughter as we dived, swam underwater and tickled in the shallows, under sheltering stones and riverside roots for rainbow trout.

In September 1935, dressed in a new grey suit and a grey cap with a red band and the school badge, I entered the mysterious portals of the Vaynor and Penderyn Grammar School, where all the teachers wore black gowns and sad serious faces. It was a world which I failed to comprehend. I was bewildered by the solemnity, the rules, the harshness, the threats and punishments. I was in detention every night and in the Autumn term of 1935 saw the sun setting over Aberdare mountain as I returned to my beloved Morning Sun. About the only thing that had any meaning for me during that Autumn was that my grandmother, who had always defended me and called me 'Yr hen lanc', died in October. She was carried in a long cortège of mourners to her last resting place in the Unitarian Hen Dy Cwrdd chapel and I lost my best friend. As Christmas approached, the Nativity story had some meaning for me too, because at the rear of the Morning Sun was my grandfather's smithy and stable. His last horse had been requisitioned by the military authorities some years earlier in the First World War. The fact that the stable had a manger made the birth of Jesus significant and meaningful to me.

After Christmas I met the formidable Mr Lovett in the corridor and probably because he had read my terminal report he said, "What's your name?". "Elwyn Bowen, Sir," I replied. "I think you have the makings of being the old man of the form," he replied. "Go to my room". He arrived, "Bend down," he said. As I did so I was propelled forward and upward and for me the term "to go into orbit" had its origins here. This I think was the beginning of my awakening. The second stage came on St. David's Day when, in the impromptu speech item, I stated that every one of the staff and the Headmaster should be incarcerated for life. I didn't say for their treatment of the children, but they clearly understood what I meant. My uncle Tom Lewis was the literary adjudicator for this 1936 Eisteddfod, and when he gave his adjudication for this open-to-all-ages event he stated, "I have to announce that the winner of the impromptu speech is my nephew, Elwyn Bowen."

This event proved to be the turning point in what up to then had been a disastrous beginning. The rest of my school days at Vaynor and Penderyn, however, proved to be the happiest, most successful and fulfilling years of my life. Acting in the school plays, playing rugby, winning the Victor Ludorum and matriculating, attending the concerts and Speech Days, remain indelibly vivid and joyous memories, shared with dedicated teachers and lovely fellow-pupils. Fresh-faced Penderyn and Pontsticill boys and smiling, pretty girls from Pontneathvaughan and Ystradfellte, flash upon that inward eye as they danced the polka and the lancers in and before the school parties at Christmas.

The more adventurous spirits, for they risked expulsion from the Grammar School for far less, sought refuge and solace after school at the billiards table of the Cefn Library. It was a venue distilled with friendship and kneaded by the mixture of local social strata which was manifested in the scholarly accents of Harry Evans B.A. B.Sc. self-taught former Maths teacher at Cyfarthfa Grammar School; in the quiet refined remarks of Gwyn Williams B.A., one of my former teachers, later to be my deputy head, and in the voices of pale-faced, scarred men with coarse hacking coughs, their lungs gasping for air, which bore testimony to the nature and unfairness of their working lives. Compared with the post-1945 era this was a cultured, perceptive people, well-read and articulate in both languages. They were an inquiring generation of people, well-versed in religion, history, politics, philosophy and literature.

These men were the remnants of a particular cultural group moulded by the terrors of trench warfare, drudgery in the mines, poverty due to large families, ill health caused by malnourishment and pneumoconiosis or tuberculosis, exacerbated by years of mass unemployment, coupled with the notorious Means Test, which ensured that a married couple with two children were allowed twenty-six shillings a week to live on. I was aware that these were a clearly defined people who had somehow survived the trauma of pre-1939 unemployed Merthyr. Scarred they may have been, but they were a kind, innocent, clean, respectable people who helped one another as far as their meagre resources would allow.

They were a brave and resilient people, so honest that neighbours left their doors unlocked by day and night.

Etched indelibly in my memory is an intensely local world, where illness and death were frequent visitors during these years of torment and poverty, when my mother, as the local nurse, provided medical assistance or advice without thought of financial reward. It was a world of lost opportunity, of the unwanted, of fainting children in school, of free boots, of shared poverty, of men carrying or wheeling coal from the 'patches', of suicides and intense suffering. Allotment associations, pigeon clubs, greyhound racing and boxing provided some cheap leisure activities. Many gained spiritual strength from the chapels and churches. The Sunday Schools attracted hundreds of children, and their outings to Barry or Porthcawl afforded days of ecstatic excitement and pleasure beyond all measure. The local libraries and Miners' Institutes provided intellectual stimulation, political inspiration and comradeship for so many of the unemployed.

The continued feeling of a shared heritage and destiny made these depressed communities strongly cohesive and supportive. Parents and local teachers recognized that the only mode of social ascent from the mire of poverty was through education. Men and women sold their houses and then paid rent to the new owners for their children to proceed to university while headmasters like John Williams in the Junior and Senior Schools, and Trevor Lovett of the Grammar School and former First World War fighter pilot, ran their respective schools with messianic dedication, with teachers whose only ambition in life appeared to be to get as many of their class as possible to score well and pass in the Scholarship Examinations.

From the late 1920s up to 1945 I attended the Sunday School with my cousins and school friends. During these lean, mean years the Sunday School under the direction of Mr Lewis Edwards, a First World War veteran and Merthyr schoolteacher, provided us with a wide range of activities in the Band of Hope, fretwork classes, Christmas parties and Sunday School trips. It is impossible to evaluate the contribution that he and his fellow Sunday School teachers made to the otherwise sad, impoverished lives of my contemporaries. Somehow these selfless Christians scratched together enough money to buy each child a book for Christmas given to them on the night of the Christmas party held in the schoolroom. This was where the famous Rev. Owen Evans and later the Reverend Hathren Davies had run the 'Pensteps Academy' from 1838 until 1901.

The annual Christmas party was an occasion of great excitement and anticipation when girls with plaited hair, sparkling eyes and smiling faces radiated sublime animation, innocence and joy of being with friends. Boys with scrubbed red faces with stiff hair parted, clean jerseys and polished shoes looked at the delicious cakes and meat sandwiches on the white clothed tables, selecting mentally what they would devour when the order was given to take their places at the tables. Where the domestic diet was often limited to bread and margarine, the cakes and meat-filled sandwiches represented a feast fit for a king. The tables, benches and settees creaked and groaned with the stretching, turning and pushing of the boisterous youngsters. The two urns simmered and steamed on the black hobs as smoke curled up the sooted chimney and red coals glowed in the grate. The lady servers, dressed in gaily patterned aprons, fussed and fed the wide-eyed happy throng. Steam poured down the old green-painted walls while sprigs of berried holly hung from the white-limed ceiling. My Sunday School teachers included one Mr Hughes who was later killed in a colliery roof fall, Hathren Jones who died at Manchester College, Oxford, and my uncle Tom Lewis (Mab y Mynydd), poet and historian.

In my early formative days at Cefn Coed and prior to my leaving in 1941 for Trinity College, the most entrancingly magic day of the year was the Sunday School trip. There were no arguments about where we should go. It was Barry and Porthcawl on alternate years. Few scholars slept on the Friday night prior to the trip. Friday was spent in preparation for the fervour of Saturday. Clothes were ironed and aired in front of the cottage fires, cakes baked in fireside ovens, hams boiled and fresh bread and cake collected from the communal bakehouses. Tempers were on a knife-edge as mothers scolded over-wrought children who could not get to sleep. Visions of golden sands, the rolling surf, the figure eight, the dodgems and the ice-cream fired the lively imagination and the black night was endless. Light streaming through threadbare curtains aroused the prone figures from their feather beds. Prods and pushes awakened the heaviest sleepers with "Come on, you'll be late for Barry". The word Barry activated the charged senses, so that children dressed, galloped down the stone winding staircases to the breakfast tables with an unusual alacrity and speed, like happy swallows coming home.

Expectant glances towards the sky with cries of "Is it fine?", "Is it raining?", "I think it will hold off", "Don't forget your coats", "You carry the sandwiches", "Where's our tickets", "Stop crying, Jim", "Your father's always the same - you can't trust him to do anything", resonated round the little kitchen until the doors opened with the agitated shouts of "The buses are there", which brought a scrum of like-minded children diving through the doors. "Stay together, don't run, wait for auntie Bessie, you'll get killed, you're on the wrong bus," fell on deaf ears.

Parents and older members sniffed the air, frowning at the dark skirmishing cloud formations. "It's alright, it's for heat," said Mrs Evans (Clean Corners). "Yes, it's just a haze," said Chris Prosser, slowly nodding to the sun. "Watch out for sunstroke," called little Miss Evans remembering what had happened to her up at Cold Knap last year when she fell asleep holding Dai's hand.

"Take your time now, children," called Mrs Jones as they fought for the best seats near the windows. Others like lemmings kneeled on the back seats, preferring a rear view of the patterned fields, grey drab villages, black pyramids of small coal on fern-clad hills and the winding gear of valley pits. Then the earth became greener, flatter and then tilted downwards towards the shimmering sea.

"There it is, it's the sea," came the cry "Where?" "Over there, can't you see it?" "Yes, I can," "It's blue", came the howl from the back. Everyone in the bus shot up, bending and weaving, with many rubbing their heads after impact with the ceiling. "Get your things together," shouted one of the exhausted mothers from the back.

We poured out of the bus with small children hanging on to their shouting mothers, older ones armed with buckets, and carrying hundredweights of sandwiches they gravitated towards the beach. "Look at the donkeys," "Look at their ears," "Watch they don't kick you". "Can I go on the donkeys mam?". "No". "Why not?". "Because I can't afford ice-cream and donkeys," was repeated a thousand times.

Soon family groups settled down on patches of sand, covered either with a cloth or newspaper. Sandwiches were unwrapped, dropped, recovered, brushed and blown to remove sand and then devoured. Nerves became frayed and any sudden movement provoked a neurotic and convulsive reaction to protect the precious food.

The afternoons were spent paddling or attempting to swim under the watchful eye of fathers parading with trousers rolled up to their knees. Occasionally, someone got lost, which resulted in a posse running in all directions. Some did this purposely so that they would end up in the 'Lost children' sector and be fed with toffees to stop them crying. I recall that one was catapulted ten feet into the air by an irate donkey for climbing on its back while it was eating its hard-earned chaff. In the evening Viv and Dewi were thrown out of the 'zoo' for tickling the snakes, while later they were severely reprimanded for sticking a pin in the headless woman's bottom. The rest of the evening was spent in the "shows" until empty pockets compelled us to leave the figure eight and the dodgems for another year.

Tired fathers and exhausted mothers carrying sleeping babies, dragging moaning toddlers, rounded up their offspring and directed them towards the buses. "That's your bus, Maggie, here's ours" or "Go and tell auntie Marie that Uncle Johnny is missing", sent another frantic dispersal of the family towards the shows and the beach. After half an hour of sorting, counting and argument, Beadle and Stevens buses departed. On board these were children sucking sticks of Barry rock, weary, weak but Barry-tanned they clutched cheap dolls and broken toys. Desperate efforts were made to catch the vomit and assuage the bad stomachs, to ease the sun-burnt backs and arms, and to comfort those so saddened that this trip to Barry Island, this jewelled eye in the memory of millions of children was gone.

It is to these days that still have a perennial freshness, to these halcyon days that old men and sad women return in their memories, seeking a lost Eden, a lost childhood of joy, excitement, escape, refuge and of peace. We have forgotten how to live - only children know the secret!

Unfortunately, as with so many school-leavers, I had no idea what to take up as a career. I had leanings towards medicine but then the decision was made for me when Mr Lovett came to my home and more or less offered me a post as apprentice chemist at Boots the Chemist in Merthyr. Alas, after many visits to Mr Lovett on my Thursday afternoons off and moaning about the boredom, the long tedious hours and the stupid customers, he suggested that I should apply to Trinity College, Carmarthen. He said, "You'll be called up for the army before long and you may be able to finish your training as a teacher there and have something to come back to after the war's over." I would have walked to Siberia to get out of Boots and duly arrived at Trinity College, Carmarthen, in September 1941.

The College was old, cold and forbidding in wartime. The rules were draconian, the rations sparse but the standard of lectures superb. Winchester College was evacuated to Trinity College and we shared lectures, Air Raid Precautions and meals in the most spartan environment imaginable. We had daily services in the College Chapel and students were trained as potential officers in the army and air force. Dozens of my fellow-students made the supreme sacrifice though I was recently disappointed to discover that there was no roll of honour at Trinity to record their deaths.

In June 1943 I was called up to the army and fortunately by then had completed my training. After demobilization in 1945 I was offered the position of temporary P.E. teacher at my old school, Vaynor and Penderyn Grammar School, in Cefn Coed.

This post involved two days at Vaynor and Penderyn and three at Brynmawr Grammar School. My salary was three pounds ten shillings a week, out of which I had to pay my train fare to and from Brynmawr. After a while in this temporary teaching post and becoming more disenchanted daily with the monotonous routine of changing my attire for gymnastics or rugby, I applied for the headship of Ystradfellte primary school, which had nineteen pupils on roll. I was not even short-listed for the post because I couldn't play the piano for the morning service. Nevertheless, I had indicated my interest in primary education and within a month was called to the telephone in the headmaster's study at Brynmawr, to be told that the Director of Education for Breconshire wanted to speak to me. "Good afternoon, Mr Bowen," he said. "Emrys Evans here. Would you be interested in taking up a temporary post as Headteacher of Llangamarch School in north Breconshire?" Without knowing where Llangamarch was, I readily agreed. When the letter of confirmation came from the Director, it was to Beulah, wherever that may have been.

Off to Beulah

I STEPPED OVER THE THRESHOLD of my cottage home, known locally as Dai Bowen's house or to those in need as Nurse Bowen's house, onto the grey pavement bright in the morning sunlight. Outside his shop, James Lloyd the grocer was sweeping the pavement, a daily chore for those enduring the unpleasantness of noise, fumes and dust on Cefn High Street. Oh for those days when Wil Danygraig walked on the pavement reading the Western Mail, while in front his horse leisurely pulled the empty cart and milk churns along the deserted High Street. No noise, no disturbance, no screeching of brakes and certainly no hurrying as he moved with the measured pace of the countryside.

By the time I had reached his grocer's shop, James Lloyd was behind the red- ribbed counter, furrowed white with his daily scrubbing. His domed, bald head capped a rotund, bespeckled face viewing a rough world with gentle blue eyes. He had what Mrs Jones, Pontycapel, called a "lovely face with a healthy complexion". He gave one the impression of a refined rural peasant, struggling to survive in an uncouth, irreligious world. I recall his spotless white overall, the sacks of Indian corn, the tubs of salted butter, emptied by a deft turn of a 'Scotch hand' and then artistically shaped by clapping the sides into a rectangle bar of gold, before the ceremonial wrapping in greaseproof paper. After fifty years, I can still scent the succulent aroma of his frying ham, not to be compared with the transparent rashers of today that exude sickening pools of fluid into the frying pan. Then of course there was Jim Lloyd's famous currant cake. It is virtually impossible to describe the flavour when newly baked. The first taste made one feel that it was so nice that it was a sin to swallow it. Many claims have been made about its mysterious qualities, ranging from its exotic Moroccan flavour, its undoubted aphrodisiac propensities, to the more mundane claim that it had spawned military successes from the Somme to the Western

Desert, or that one portion could energize a good collier to cut forty tons of anthracite in a day! It was further claimed that Jim Lloyd had thrown away thousands of pounds by refusing to disclose his secret recipe. As he stated, "An artist or a composer like Joseph Parry only needs to make one great creation and I feel the same way about my cake."

After thanking him for his good wishes, I stepped soundlessly over the sawdust newly covering the flag-stoned floor and proceeded under the railway bridge, acknowledging the flippant advice of George Ablett, landlord of the Drovers' Arms when he stated, "You watch those country girls, Elwyn boy."

"Never mind about the country girls," I retorted. "Is it right what Johnny Morning Sun says about the Public analyst's report on your beer?"

"What was that?" he asked, rather perplexed, "I've heard nothing about it."

"Well," I added, "he says the analyst's report on your beer stated 'this horse should not do any further heavy work'."

Before he had collected his thoughts for a final salvo at me, I had disappeared around the corner onto the Station Plain where in 1831 my ancestor Dafydd Lewis had saved the life of Mr Kins, surgeon to the 93rd Highland Regiment when the Cefn rioters thought that he'd come to arrest Lewis. They forced the surgeon to kneel in prayer before being shot. They removed his sword and were about to shoot him when Dafydd Lewis staggered from his white-washed cottage and called, "Let him go, boys, he's just removed the musket-ball from my shoulder and, furthermore, his wife's dying in Brecon."

Reflecting upon this dramatic incident, I opened the yellow gate leading onto the long platform of the Cefn Station where two men appeared in deep discussion. One was Harry Evans B.A., a retired Cyfarthfa Grammar School teacher, and a stranger obviously waiting for the train which would take me to Beulah. Harry Evans, white-haired, tall, ruddy-faced, had graduated from a tough quarter of Georgetown to become a Maths teacher. By studying under the flickering candlelight in one of the ironworkers' cottages he had attained a position of authority in the Cyfarthfa Grammar School. His two degrees reflected the strength of his body and intellect and this was still visible in his erect posture. He stood waving his fishing rod as if conducting an invisible choir, as he emphasized some point that he was making to the slender, dark- haired stranger of rather younger years.

"Ah, this is Mr Elwyn Bowen," said Harry Evans. This made me feel rather important because he normally referred to me by my Christian name. My new position undoubtedly entitled me to this greater respect!

"He's off to Beulah to become a Headmaster," asserted Harry Evans. "Let me introduce you to the former Art Master at Cyfarthfa, Mr Williams," he added. I saw a man whose outward appearance was that of a person gentle and refined, dark-eyed and intelligent in his manner and speech.

"Well, that's interesting," he said, "I am going to Garth, the next village. You'll know my brother-in-law no doubt - Trevor Davies, formerly of the Pentwyn Inn, Dolygaer."

"Yes, I knew Trevor very well," I added. I did not extend the conversation about Trevor because I was aware that there had been some problem, something to do originally with the loss of the Pentwyn Inn due to the expansion of the Dolygaer reservoir with the consequent loss of the family home and farm.

I excused myself and made for the iron Victorian urinal that had witnessed the very beginning of rail transport in this part of the world. I smiled as I heard Harry Evans extolling the virtues of the Coch-y-bonddu artificial fly in a stentorian voice that obliterated the morning rumble of industry at Merthyr. He had the observable appearance and oratorical fluency of one trained and experienced through the chapel and school. He was given to emphasizing explicitly some incident reinforced by gesture and expressive glances and pauses. Mr Williams was nodding in assent as he had probably done for years, in the staffroom at Cyfarthfa. 'Sheepy' Evans, as he was affectionately known, had been married three times and his last wife, half his seventy- five years was attractive and Welsh-speaking; she was from Llanstephan, in Carmarthenshire. This Welsh 'Mr Chips' comprehensively represented the dignity, prestige and status of pre-World War II Grammar School teachers.

The toot of the whistle and the puffing of the engine brought Harry Evans, his companion and myself nearer to the brink of the platform. 'Abernant', black as soot, steaming and screeching, braked to a standstill. Water dripped from the oil-covered flanks of this seething monster as we boarded one of the three carriages. One would have been ample as there were only three other passengers aboard. I sat facing forward so that I could look down the High Street, and this enabled me in a few moments to wave to my parents standing rather sadly outside our home. The lady sitting opposite me acknowledged me and recognizing that I wasn't sure of her, reminded me that I had worked with her daughter, Peggy Evans, some three years previously when my career as a pharmaceutical chemist at Boots came to a sudden end.

By now we were nearly in Pontsarn, passing the massive Vaynor quarries belching smoke and dust into the morning air. One passenger stood forlornly on the platform at Pontsarn station and I remembered the comment made by the Reverend J.E. Jenkins, rector of this parish of Vaynor, when he wrote in the last century, "Today with its Pontsarn and Coed-y-Cymmer and its twenty-one passenger trains coming and going daily, Vaynor is in the world and the world has come to Vaynor". How right he was – nine thousand tickets were issued in the first month of opening the line in 1867.

Pontsarn nestled under the awesomely beautiful cliffs of the Morlais Castle, lying deep in the Taf Fechan gorge, surrounded by masses of majestic hardwood trees and glades of pristine beauty. The silent retreat was disturbed on this lovely morning only by the roar of the boiling cauldron of foam and spray cascading over the eroded rocks into Pwll Glas. Everything sublime in nature, mountain brooks, great oaks weathered by centuries, lofty peaks, hedgerows run wild and field flowers, cradling white-washed farmhouses, may at once be found here, austerely and sublimely mysterious and wonderful.

My reverie was interrupted by Mrs Evans, who was gazing down towards the Vaynor Church on the other side of the river.

"Is it correct that two French armies fought against each other over there?" she asked, pointing in the direction of the church.

I nodded in agreement. "Yes," I said, "as strange at it might seem, two French armies fought there, at Maes-y-faenor and around the church destroyed in 1291."

"You mentioned that the church was destroyed," she added.

"Yes, the old church was destroyed but in 1295 the Vaynorians built a new one. Only the tower now stands, and the other church is the one built in 1870 and paid for by R.T. Crawshay, the Cyfarthfa ironmaster," I replied.

"Was he buried there?" she asked.

"Yes, R.T. Crawshay died 10th May 1879, and lies in a grave nearby with a memorial stone weighing eleven tons, and measuring about eleven feet by seven with the words 'God forgive me' inscribed thereon."

"I was just saying to Mr Evans that the Pentwyn Inn and the reservoir attracted thousands of visitors annually in the last century," said Mr Williams.

"Yes," I agreed, "and that spirit of enterprise was strong in one Frederick Atkins during the years 1864 to 1865 when he brought a steamboat to the Brecon Beacons".

"I've never heard of that," shouted Harry Evans.

"Not for long," I replied. "Misfortune struck in the late winter of 1866-7 when during a violent storm it sank in thirty feet of water."

"Is it still down there?" asked Harry Evans.

"No, Thomas Jepson, a Dowlais contractor, without the aid of divers using pulleys and tackle, raised her in June 1867, after she'd been submerged for several months. In less than two hours she was able to take a trial run around the reservoir and, under the command of Captain Atkins, made regular voyages round Pentwyn reservoir until he died in December 1869. He was an eccentric, exceptionally kind and, towards the close of his life, lived alone in a hut near Pontsticill. His only companions were two monkeys and a vixen," I informed the old teacher.

The toot of the whistle indicated that we were approaching Dolygaer Station. Harry Evans, obviously either eager to get away from all this doubtful history, or to get on the reservoir, was already on his feet with his bag slung over his shoulder and cane rod ready in his hand. The train crunched to a stop, Harry opened the door, and turning to me said, "Good luck in your new job."

It was said that to work at Torpantau a man needed to be a little mad. Even the sunshine of high summer does not dispel the loneliness, and to work here in winter with snow and rainstorms sweeping across a landscape devoid of trees or shelter demanded a cast-iron fortitude. This vast tract of unenclosed common brooded brown over a sombre stretch of prehistoric barrows and hollows, haggard and majestic in its simplicity. Solitude gazed from the untameable wilderness of heath, distilled by the scorching sun in summer, and eroded by tempests in winter. From the beginning of time, it had worn the same dull-brown garment, unchanged except by snow which brought with it silence and serenity. Loneliness and mystery gazed out of its countenance, intensely pure and invulnerable. This great, inviolate wasteland possessed an ancient permanence as unaltered as the stars above the Beacons, the haunt of the falcon by day and of demons by night.

It was seven miles from Torpantau to Talybont, an incline with a gradient of 1 in 38; the descent from Torpantau was as exhilarating as it was magnificent. The Spring fields, some newly ploughed, others resplendent with meadow flowers surrounded by hedgerows fresh with green, ran wild. On we sped through Talybont and as I gazed across the mist of the valley, I could plainly see Llansantffraed Church where Henry Vaughan the Silurist was buried. As the train pulled out of Talybont, my thoughts were interrupted by Mr Williams who said, "Don't forget, we change at Talyllyn." We changed trains and in a very short time were speedily heading for Builth.

My knowledge of Builth was limited to the fact that I knew that the wells there had curative properties and that Llewelyn ap Gruffudd, the last Welsh Prince, had been killed at nearby Cilmeri in 1282.

The intermittent toot of the train's whistle announced our approach to Builth station. "We've arrived at Builth," said Mr Williams as he collected a small leather case, suggesting but a brief stay at Cwm Graig Ddu at Garth. "We have to go the rest of the way by bus," he said as we left the station. There waiting for the train was George Shuter's green bus, small, utilitarian in the extreme with iron-framed seats covered with the thinnest possible layer of green imitation leather. After we had paid our respective fares, the engine started with a violence that made the windows rattle and the seats to shake almost in despair at another journey. He drove with speed, weaving through congested streets, throwing Williams and myself from side to side and when he braked, I felt my stomach hurtling through the windscreen. People scurried, cars and vans pulled into the side, and a way was quickly and spontaneously cleared for George's bus, as it lurched and careered through crowds of onlookers who sought refuge in the shops and taverns.

"It's Builth Fair today," exclaimed Mr Williams as he returned breathlessly to his seat after orbiting the bus. As a matter of fact, for some minutes I am sure that he had actually left the bus and returned through one of the half-open windows. "Big day in Builth today," one of the most important days...," he muttered before taking another flight. I gazed out of the window when the road became blocked with a herd of lowing Herefords. On the crowded pavements children enchanted with the throngs of men, obviously farmers or farm labourers with faces red with blood, black- bowlered or sporting caps askew on their heads, sauntered along, joking and shouting to friends. Others with hair stiff and unruly due to exposure to wind and rain, gossiped in groups leaning on home-made crooks or walking sticks, while others sped purposefully along the crowded pavements, carrying willow baskets, tools or utensils under their arms. Children clutching dolls or packets of sweets were dragged reluctantly from shop to shop by black-coated, robust women, intent on making the most of this one day's respite from the unending toil of farmwork.

A country fair has traditionally been one of the brightest events in the calendar of rustic life. It was a day anxiously anticipated as some unique jubilee, one of the few free days allotted to the farm servant, a day of unrestrained festivity. It was a blissful day, a cessation of labour when for a few hours the humble man became his own master. This freedom was reflected in the gaiety of spirit, the laughter and the greetings. Younger spirits bestowed special care upon their dress and appearance. Clearly apparent was the studied neatness of their attire, the jauntiness of their walk or the smiling glance that could result in a betrothal. It was therefore a day of radiant expectation, a day that could illuminate the future, a day of destiny or disappointment.

This was a day of hiring and of new masters and mistresses, of buying blankets, trousers and boots, seeds and tools, of selling cattle, pigs, ponies and pups, butter, eggs and poultry, sheep and lambs. A day of business and of leisure. These were a people proud of their ancestors, their farms, their stock, their customs and traditions; wedded to the soil and a way of life lost in the deep mists of time. This day was for many a welcome rupture of the monotony of deadly loneliness and frustration, engendered by isolation from human communication and society. The sound of silence can be as sickening as it is beautiful. The beauty of the countryside is truly in the eye of the beholder, but there is another hidden frontier that only those who live on remote farms and in lonely places understand. This is why the fair day is such a very special occasion in rural life.

The beaming faces, the full taverns and busy shops were soon disappearing as we wove our way from the town centre, and raced through the little village of Cilmeri, passing the obelisk commemorating Llywelyn ap Gruffudd, and on to Garth. To our left was a long range of bare hills. White-washed farmsteads clung amid sycamores and oaks to the moor-capped Epynt which was strung along the valley. A small two- classroomed school suggested a habitation and village with a few houses of simple proportions and a village hall and post office.

"I leave you now. This is Garth," said Mr Williams as he dismounted and walked towards a waiting car. He immediately struck up a short conversation with a young man who turned and waved. It was my former school friend, Trevor Davies, formerly of the Pentwyn Inn at Dolygaer. Memories of faces, voices, pupils, teachers, classrooms and speech days filled with pride, expectation and awe flooded through my mind, reminding me of carefree days. The bus jerked me from my reverie as we passed yet another large country house with lodge and drive called Garth House. One of the daughters, Sarah Gwynne, I recalled, had married Charles Wesley.

We soon passed Llanlleonfel Church standing gaunt and silhouetted against the horizon on my left, and within a few minutes the old bus shuddered to an abrupt stop outside the shop at Beulah. George Shuter smilingly turned to me and said, "This is Beulah. Good luck to you. I'll see you Friday around 3.30 in the afternoon if you're going home."

I thanked him, dismounted and waited until he had disappeared around the bend of the road as he proceeded to Llanwrtyd four miles away. As I stood and glanced around the deserted village, I noticed that it was blessed with two double-fronted shops, a bridge, a few cottages and a Post Office. It was at this moment that I stepped back in time. I had discovered another culture, centuries old, peaceful and tranquil, a calm retreat from the busy industrial village of Cefn Coed.

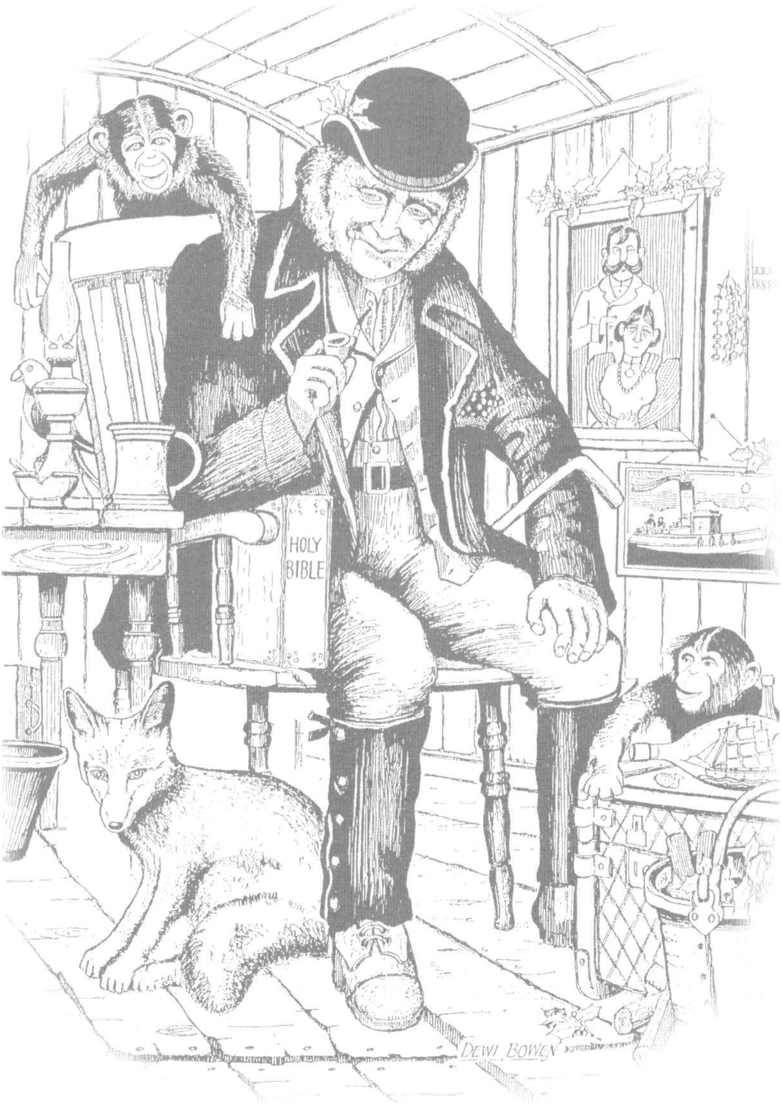
HOLY
BIBLE
DEWI BOWEN

The New School

A GOOD-LOOKING, WAVY-HAIRED, tall lady appeared on the doorstep of the house adjoining the Post Office opposite.

"Mr Bowen," she said. "I'm Miss Morgan. Come in."

She led the way along a dimly lit passage to the living room.

"Sit down," she said. "I'll make a cup of tea. I'm sure you could do with one."

She disappeared into the small back-kitchen and reappeared with tea and Welsh cakes.

"Eat away, there's plenty in there," she said.

"They'll only go waste because I shall be leaving for my home at Ystradgynlais tonight, to take up my new post as Head of Cynlais Infants' School tomorrow morning."

She then gave me a résumé of her career with particular reference to Beulah School, its number on roll and information about my assistant, Miss Blodwen Morgan, who had taught there for over thirty years and who lodged with Miss Parry just across the river from where we were. She mentioned that the eleven plus examination results would be out soon and that one pupil, Brynwyn Griffiths, would have done well.

"Take your case up to Mrs Jones Wylfa and when you've unpacked come back and I'll show you the School before I leave," she added.

I thanked her for my refreshments and assured her that I would return as soon as possible. Genial Miss Morgan indicated how I should find my lodgings at Wylfa. I carried my suitcase along the road to my left; the other led over an iron bridge spanning the Camarch river. I passed some nineteenth-century white-washed cottages, one of which I discovered later housed Bill Cobbler, the shoe-maker. A few yards around the bend of the road I encountered a wheelwright's shop with an array of newly painted cartwheels leaning against the detached workshop. From within resounded the thud of hammer blows and then, with slow steps, a grey-haired sixty-year-old man guided a newly made, unpainted wheel through the open oak door.

"Good afternoon, are you looking for someone?" he asked. He pointed out my destination after introducing himself as "Dai Arthur the wheelwright", whose daughter was the Headteacher at Garth, the village I had passed through some twenty minutes previously.

"I live in the cottages by Llanlleonfel Church with my daughter. The other daughter is married to George Shuter the bus driver," he added. "And she lives up at Llanwrtyd four miles away." I moved to the open door and gazed inside, into the workshop of a traditional craftsman with its uneven bench, vices, tools and an earthen floor strewn with wood shavings. From inside came the pungent fragrance of timber- scented air, cob-webbed walls and roof timbers mellowed by the damp earth underfoot. Stacked against the walls were blocks of ash, elm and oak which, after years of seasoning, would under his skilled hands and perceptive eye, be shaped into felloes, spokes and wheel rims. I dragged myself away from the craft workshop, promising to return as soon as possible to satisfy my overwhelming desire to seek out some of the secrets of a craft that was entirely new to me. Clearly this craft was of crucial importance to the economy of the countryside.

I reluctantly turned from this dextrous craftsman whose countenance bespoke a scriptural tranquillity, responding undoubtedly to the satisfaction derived from his trade, which carried the intrinsic satisfaction of witnessing a complete creation in the form of a gambo which carried a lifetime guarantee. He was a far cry from the factory worker described as 'alienated' by Karl Marx, because they merely made parts without the fulfilment and joy of seeing and creating the finished article. Dai Arthur, with his wrinkled brow, furrowed chin, stubbled cheeks and watery blue eyes exemplified the typical, highly skilled rural craftsman, now unfortunately made redundant by modern technology, the demise of horse-drawn vehicles and an economy no longer inspired by rural self-sufficiency.

I soon arrived at the Carpenters' Arms with its five green windows, old door, swinging sign and stone-flagged passage, ending in a staircase. It was a typical wayside inn, evoking even in Springtime the enchanting dream of a Dickensian Christmas spent here. I imagined weary travellers dismounting from snow-covered stage-coaches, entering the crowded kitchen, filled with the sweet aroma of roasting beef on a white-clothed table, resplendent with boiled and roasted meats, pigeon pie, boiled hams, muffins and cakes. Of weather-beaten-faced drivers with broad-brimmed black hats, coloured waistcoats under thick red coats and high black boots. Proud men drinking warm portations of rum and beaming benignly in response to the many tips and drinks which they had received.

A man carrying a sack of goods from the village shop caught my eye as he came round the bend of the road. I walked on until I came to a red-bricked, detached house bearing the name Wylfa. I was greeted by a short pleasant lady who introduced herself as Mrs Alfred Jones. I entered through the back door and the smell of paraffin burning in the kitchen stove. This was yet another clear indication that I was stepping back in time, from when we had used a paraffin lamp at home. This, incidentally, had been considered one step up from candle-light but still lower in status to electric light, found only with the middle classes of Cefn Coed in the 1930s. After an exchange of the usual courtesies, I gathered that Mrs Jones had two daughters, one of whom was a teacher in Newport, and a husband who was a carpenter on the Llwyn Madoc Estate.

Soon footsteps and the opening of the back-kitchen door, indicated the arrival of Mr Alfred Jones.

"Alfred, Mr Bowen is in here," called Mrs Jones from the front room.

He came slowly into the room with its black leather-covered sofa under the window, its oak table and chairs, sideboard and pictures of people long dead. In Alfred Jones I recognized a man, studious in appearance and dressed in dungarees, black working boots and cap. His dark, furrowed brow, deep-set eyes, and perfect Welsh exemplified the class of natural scholars who by circumstances and time had unfairly missed out on educational opportunity, and as a result had wasted their talents "on the desert air". Nevertheless, this class of men, often rural craftsmen, were the natural leaders of their communities, holding posts of responsibility in the local chapels and churches, on eisteddfod committees and as representatives on Parish, District or County Councils. Others were poets and musicians who gained prestige and status from winning at eisteddfodau. By virtue of his skill as an estate carpenter, chapel leader and poet, Alfred Jones personified a traditional wise man of the Welsh countryside.

The room with its polished, antique furniture, corner cupboard stacked with treasured half-sets of china, the loud tick-tock of the grandfather clock, the brass fire- tongs beside the unlit fire, the brown-beamed ceiling, the variegated geraniums lining the windowsill, and the pungent smell of paraffin and the soft lilting cadences of Alfred Jones's speech, created a refined and gentle aura of rural tranquillity. My bedroom bore all the evidence of cleanliness and freshness. It was a typical Thomas Hardy cottage with its woodstore at the rear and weed-free garden. Everything suggested care, precision and organization stemming from a strictly limited income, a peasant simplicity, and the Nonconformist ethic honesty coupled with hard work and respectability. This restricted life-style was not totally alien to the chapel life of the South Wales valleys, but it represented an entirely different culture emanating from the almost medieval power of the squire and his patronage. The servility and acceptance of this traditional heritage, without audible complaint, was almost identical to the state of affairs associated with the ironmasters and coal-owners of the eighteenth and nineteenth centuries.

One of the first questions put to me by my landlord was "Oh, you're from the works." This was repeated so often that I began to suspect an inference to some inferior race, and indeed one person stated, "Whenever I travel to Cardiff I see women leaning on their brushes gossiping to their neighbours on the pavement."

The statement was so perverted and untrue that it clearly demonstrated the degree of misunderstanding between the cultures where the women, the unsung heroines of the valleys, were up at four in the morning before sending husbands and sons to the pits and still up at midnight airing clothes and all too frequently mourning the frequent deaths and injuries of their loved ones. This attitude towards people of the valleys was frequently reinforced when others, referring to Jim Evans the Post Office, so sarcastically and disparagingly stated, "He's from the works." We were both obviously of another culture.

After answering a welter of questions relating to my home, my family and my religion, it became clear that they were formulating a character sketch of me and wondering probably whether I fitted the traditional stereotype of a rural village schoolmaster. I was quite satisfied that I had given a satisfactory report, but there was something sinister in the fact that I came from "the works". I left soon to meet Elizabeth Morgan and found her waiting for me and I apologized for the delay. Our conversation was interrupted by the continuous screams of large birds swooping and gliding over the village and vanishing as they descended into the surrounding fields. "You have a lot of birds here," I commented.

"Oh! they are curlews and come here annually, this is their breeding ground," she replied.

"I'm amazed to see so many," I answered, "because I normally only hear or see a solitary curlew on the moorland of the Beacons." We left her home and crossed the bridge over the Camarch. We stopped and listened to the casually flowing stream, as it idly formed whirlpools against the dark vegetation lying under the overhanging alder- trees. In a flash, I caught the luminous rainbow colours of a green-headed kingfisher as it sped over the bridge, weaving to and fro under the branches.

"We'll call in Miss Parry's now," she said, "and you can meet Miss Morgan." She turned to a wooden gate leading to one of the more modern semi-detached red- brick houses owned by the estate. She knocked on the front door and opened it with a shout of "Hello, Miss Parry, Miss Morgan here, I've brought Mr Bowen to meet you." With that a short white-haired elderly lady appeared, her face red, her eyes radiating kindliness and warmth. Her shoulders draped in a Welsh flannel shawl of some antiquity was loosely wrapped round her diminutive frame hidden by a coloured apron. She dropped her hand from her mouth and welcomed me over the threshold into the spacious living room. Sitting cosily at the side of the coal fire was a lady of about fifty with greying hair and a cigarette drooping from her mouth. She nodded involuntarily; this suggested possibly a form of nervous disorder associated with Parkinson's disease. She addressed me in Welsh, "Sut mae, Mr Bowen? Croeso gynnes i Beulah". I responded rather diffidently, aware of my limited linguistic skills in front of three fluent Welsh-speakers. I felt a surge of warmth and welcome within the walls and was unaware then that I was to spend six delightful years under that roof.

We left and ascended the steep hill leading towards Llwyn Madoc Non- Provided School, leaving behind us the little cluster of houses and the sounds of children rejoicing with infectious laughter, as they tickled for fish in the stone-strewn stream while others performed feats of dangerous acrobatics on their old bicycles. As we left the village, the curlew cries were interrupted by the strident, continuous, heavy thuds of metal upon metal. This sound intensified as we proceeded, and then a black-aproned, black-capped man appeared swinging a sledgehammer at a wheel held firmly to the ground by Dai Arthur the wheelwright. "That's Mr Mathias, the blacksmith, with Mr Arthur," said Miss Morgan. They paused for a moment as Mr Mathias wiped his perspiring face with his torn cap. He smiled, revealing large white teeth contrasting visibly with his soot-blackened countenance. He touched his forelock, "Hello, Miss Morgan, we're working late tonight banding a wheel." Then he turned to me and said, "I won't shake hands with you because they're dirty." I took his hand nevertheless, and felt his power crushing mine in a vice-like grip, grinding my bones painfully together. Meanwhile, Dai Arthur was creating clouds of smoke and steam by throwing buckets of water over the newly banded wheel. "That's it," he said. "I'll collect it tomorrow Jim." He again politely touched his cap, retreated into the dark smithy to pick up a bag used for carrying his midday meal, turned and, smiling, nodded to us before departing homewards. "We're going too," exclaimed Miss Morgan. I felt for the second time that day an intense urge to stay to ask questions and to probe the mystery of this ancient craft. "I'll be back, Mr Mathias, as soon as possible", I exclaimed as we left wondering what the school was like. "Fancy taking up an appointment, even a temporary one, in the wilds of mid-Wales without ever seeing the place let alone the school. I must be mad," I muttered to myself.

Meditations about my foolishness were soon dispelled by the evensong of thrushes, blackbirds and the ever-sad curlew cries floating low over the hedges that were filled with hazel catkins, black ash buds profusely carpeted beneath by greater celandines and wood sorrel. Rising to the darkening upland horizon was a patched landscape of lush green that was speckled with cattle and sheep. An ascending spiral of smoke bending in the wind suggested a farmhouse hidden by sheltering sycamores and there suddenly, behind the signpost, only partially visible behind some noble beeches, proud but savaged by many winters, lay the country school black, brooding and silent.

Two large-windowed classrooms joined by a long room at the rear faced south onto an uneven, earthen yard with grassy patches and dead tree-trunks separated by tufts of rushes, all bounded by hedges run wild. A slated canopy attached to the infants' classroom to the right afforded some shelter for the forty or so children, including some evacuees from Bootle. Some walked up to three miles along mountain paths purposely strewn with coloured glass to guide them to this hundred-year-old seat of rural learning. The windows, burnished now by the setting sun, sparkled and enlivened the building, languishing undisturbed by the animated cries of children bubbling with the joy of young creatures unaware of their futures.

The crunch of our feet upon the granulated path, worn rough

by rain and feet, disturbed two pheasants nesting in the rushes. The rising red-breasted, blue-tailed cock screamed his discontent as he sped hot-footed across the yard and rose with a flurry of feathers, thrashing the air then crashing through the topmost branches of the hedge, seeking safety from our impious presence at this mystic hour, when birds and denizens of hedge and moor prepare for the night.

"Let's go inside," said Miss Morgan, "because the time's getting on and I have to leave for Ystradgynlais." Using an enormous key, she unlocked the door and we entered what was to be my classroom. I found it to be a spacious room with a tortoiseshell coal-fired boiler, a wooden floor, a teacher's desk, an old piano, yellow- painted walls and green-framed windows. From the classroom I could recognize the faint outline of the Epynt mountain visible between the budding beech-trees at the entrance to the yard. The infants' room was a replica of my room, both joined by a longer room called 'the hall'. Possibly because of its relative antiquity and sepulchral silence, it carried a sense of sadness and desertion and an echo of footsteps and personalities that had occupied this place as children. "Thank you for showing me around Miss Morgan," I said. "We'd better go because you have a long journey to make."

"One other thing," she said. "Idwal Jones lives in the school house, he's the son of Mrs Jones Dolaeron, who brings the milk to school in the mornings." She locked the school and soon we were out of the yard and walking back to the village some quarter of a mile away to the south.

I left my lodgings at half past-eight the following morning and walked towards the school, passing boys and girls talking in groups as they too went in the same direction. At nine o'clock my assistant, Miss Blodwen Morgan, called them in and we marked our respective registers before bringing them all into my room for assembly. I had never, apart from my brief spells of teaching practice at Trinity College, ever taught children as young as four, neither had I ever contemplated teaching twenty-six children in the age range of seven to fourteen years of age in the same room.

The organization of desks and their sizes reflected this age-range. Two blackboards were daily filled with sums for the respective classes, and while I taught one age-group something new every morning, the others proceeded with the work on the blackboards. Some lessons, however, were provided for the whole class. The class that was regarded as the most important was the scholarship class. These were children who were given two chances at ten and eleven-plus to try the entrance examination to the grammar school at Builth. The examination comprised four papers, two in English and two in Mathematics or Arithmetic as it was then called.

The first English paper was an essay or composition with a time allowance of one hour and a choice of about five topics. The second English paper was a general grammar paper, which required a thorough knowledge of parts of speech, singulars and plurals and the like. The first arithmetic paper was a mechanical arithmetic paper, which involved using the four rules i.e. addition, subtraction, multiplication and division of such topics as number, money, weight, time and capacity. The second paper was a problem paper and could cause difficulties. In addition, it was necessary to know the tables thoroughly in order to compute, and similarly a great deal of time was given to writing compositions, spelling and grammar. I soon discovered, too, that teachers were assessed for promotion by their scholarship results and that Miss Arthur, daughter of Dai Arthur the wheelwright at Beulah, was highly regarded as the Headteacher at Garth where she had around twenty pupils. Homework was an essential element in all this preparation for the scholarship.

I recall with considerable pride that Philip Price, son of the village carpenter, Cyril Price, was awarded top place in the Builth area when only ten years of age, and that the scholarship results for the area were cancelled one year, probably around 1948 when I queried their accuracy. I was delighted to receive a letter from Mr Emrys Evans, the Director of Education for Breconshire, which stated, "It is a very fortunate circumstance for your pupil Margaret Powell that you queried her result, because it has been found that she scored fifty-one marks out of sixty on Arithmetic paper B, and that the examiner in drawing a circle around the marks went through the figure one. Unfortunately for her, she was only awarded five marks out of sixty instead of fifty- one. She is now placed fifth in the order of merit for entry to Builth Grammar School. Philip Price went on to become a Bank Manager and Margaret Powell a very highly qualified nurse. By a strange coincidence Cyril Price and I had been in the army together in 1943.

It was customary to have two teachers in most country schools, a qualified headteacher and frequently an unqualified infants' teacher. My assistant, Miss Morgan, was a brilliant teacher and came under the category of "supplementary" teacher. She had been teaching since she had left Grammar School at fourteen and was earning about two pounds a week. During my six years at Beulah, I did not receive one child from her who was not a fluent reader at seven years of age. Her method of teaching was by phonics, whereby the children were drilled in the sounds of the letters which were then combined to read the words. Many years later I became head of one of the largest schools in Wales and employed five remedial teachers. These were fully engaged in trying to teach Junior School children to read who had failed at the infant level, mainly due to modern methods of teaching the subject.

After a few weeks with Mr and Mrs Jones, Wylfa, I moved and went into lodgings with Miss Parry and Miss Morgan, both of whom mothered me and made my sojourn at Beulah a period of sheer delight. Keeping a pig, making butter and cheese, keeping a cow and chickens were a form of life that was entirely new to me. I learned the secrets of feeding, killing and salting a pig. Miss Parry was an expert at salting, using just the right amount of salt and saltpetre to produce a taste on the bacon and ham that can hardly be imagined today. This is one of the many secrets that the gwerin passed on to their children and, regrettably all too frequently, took to the grave with them.

Miss Parry was unable to sell me any of her home-produced

butter, because it was secretly purchased by her own trusted customers. This was a time of post-war food rationing and it was an offence to buy butter, eggs, cheese, meat or bacon on what was known as the Black Market. There was an abundance of home-produced food locally, and I made some general enquiries as to where I might be able to purchase some butter and eggs to take down to my family in Cefn. I was advised to contact the Vicar's mother, Mrs Hawkins, who might be able to help with the eggs! So after a week at Beulah I visited Mrs Hawkins on a Tuesday evening for a preliminary talk prior to my going home on the following Friday.

My visit to the Vicarage took me northwards through the village, and the fact that the entrance to the Vicarage parkland was guarded by a single-storey lodge suggested that the vicar had held a prestigious position in the local life of nineteenth- century parishioners in this benefice. This impression was confirmed by the size of the Vicarage, a spacious Victorian edifice with a columned entrance and immense door. When opened by Mrs Hawkins it groaned on its black grid-iron hinges and revealed a wide staircase and long corridor urgently in need of decoration. The walls revealed yellow paint curling in flakes from the damp white plaster beneath. Rooms closed by heavy doors, likewise patterned by age, hid the former glory of morning rooms, studies and parlours that once enjoyed the polite talk of the local middle classes, graced by the presence of members of the local squirearchy. Heavy brocaded curtains, bleached by sun and dampness, hung limply over cobwebbed dirty windows. Old wallpaper on bare walls still scowled at the wanton neglect of its former Victorian glory.

The cold feel of decaying walls and woodwork pervaded the dark shadows until I was ushered into a rear room warmed by a coal fire, in a typical parlour grate of nineteenth-century vintage, cracked and disfigured by long winter fires that sought to bring some little comfort to this forbiddingly cold abode. Flames hued in purples, yellows and reds twisted, fought and rose in the ascending puffs of smoke that were reflected in dancing shadows that wove and spun on the dimly lit walls of this vast room. Lounging large and ugly on a rag mat before the welcoming fire was an immense bull mastiff. He lifted his flattened snout protruding from his furrowed face and rose on four spreadeagled legs, menacingly ready to propel himself at my vulnerable body. As I recoiled before the deep-chested growl, the bared fangs and provocative posture of this fearful creature, a vociferous command thundered from the shadows, "Down, Prince, down!" Reluctantly, he cowered and slunk harmlessly under the table. The Vicar rose from the fireside chair and introduced himself.

"I'm Brinley Hawkins, how are you?" A black-suited, cherubic, red-faced man of twenty-seven to thirty years of age, portly and polished, stood before me and invited me to join him by the fireside. During our long and pleasant conversation, I discovered that he had been a curate in the Swansea valley and Sennybridge, and more importantly that we were both related to the Jordans of Pontardawe. His mother, now in her early seventies, bore the hallmarks of hard work and struggle in her care-worn face. She was evidently proud of her son's promotion and of his ascendancy to relative middle- classness. This status as Vicar of Eglwys Oen Duw carried a warm friendship with Commander Evan Thomas, squire of Llwyn Madoc. She now moved confidently, finding her feet socially in this community, long accustomed to revering both clergy and gentry.

The quietude and repose of the stone-flagged, lamp-lit room was rather mysteriously disturbed by the muted clucking of hens and the raucous fanfare of a cockerel. These sounds appeared to be descending from heaven upon this small gathering. Occasionally these strident notes pierced the gloom and disturbed and excited the dog. He displayed his annoyance with a loud roar of disapproval. I wondered whether I had left the front-door open and that some inquisitive feathered friends might have sought shelter and wandered into the elongated passage outside. My interpretation, however, was corrected by Mrs Hawkins when she declared, "We are breeding Golden Leg Bar chickens upstairs."

"Oh," I said, not knowing much about chickens other than that they laid eggs.

"Yes, these are a very special breed," she said. Again this meant little to me other than perhaps they produced more, bigger or more expensive eggs. The reference to eggs afforded the opportunity to broach the question, "Do they produce many eggs?" An affirmative "Yes," encouraged me then to fence no longer and to ask, "Do you think, Mrs Hawkins, you could spare me a few eggs to take home over the weekend?" "Yes, of course I can," she replied, "and in any case you're in the family." Whether this statement was to ease her conscience or mine I never bothered to find out. "Thank you, Mrs Hawkins," I replied. "Can I come up on Thursday to collect them?" I asked. "Yes, I'll have them ready for you and would you like me to ask Mrs Edwards, Aberannell, that's the farm just outside", she said as she gestured with her hand to indicate its proximity, "for a few pounds of butter for you. Would you like some?" I responded with delight, "Yes, please, I would be very grateful for as much as you can obtain," I added and to give some sort of credibility I stated, "My brother is a Bevin Boy, working underground in Elliotts Colliery, New Tredegar ... this butter ... this extra nourishment would be a Godsend." "Come and meet Mrs Edwards before you leave," she said, and guided me out through the rear door to the wooden bridge over the Annell brook which separated the Vicarage from the farmhouse.

She took me across the little footbridge and through the farm fold to the side door. "Hello, Mrs Edwards, I'm here," she called. "I've brought Mr Bowen the new school teacher with me." It was now dark and the open door disclosed a farmhouse kitchen, traditional with its black-leaded fire and sham grate. It had a cooking oven on one side, boiler with brass tap on the other and a black kettle hanging from a chimney chain. Above was a mantelshelf with variously sized brass candlesticks and a brass rod suspended below carried neatly ironed clothes. Overhead a cord line traversed the kitchen ceiling also supporting clothes airing for the family.

Mrs Edwards was in her late sixties and a rather small woman of delicate mould with her white hair neatly tied in a bun. Her brown eyes were clear, honest and searching. She was truly unpretentious, sociable and polite.

"Mr Bowen is wondering whether you could sell him some butter to take home to his family in South Wales," asked Mrs Hawkins.

"Yes, when would you like some and how much would you like?" she asked.

"Well, I could collect it on Thursday evening and I could do with about three pounds please."

"I think I could manage that amount by Thursday night," she replied. "But don't tell anyone you've had it from me," she added. "The Food Inspector has taken a lot of people to court. I heard today that he's been enquiring about people using flour for making bread for themselves instead of giving it to their pigs. Oh, I'm sorry, please sit down", and her outstretched hand guided me towards the high-backed settle by the fire.

"No, I won't tell anyone," I replied. "I'm just glad to be able to get it for my family," I added without fully realizing that I was involving myself in transparent law-breaking. I felt, however, that there was nothing shameless or reprehensible in acquiring food for my family. While totally and shamefully inexperienced and naïve in these business transactions, and without reflecting too deeply on the matter, I agreed. In any case, if it was acceptable to the Vicar's mother to sell me eggs and negotiate on my behalf there couldn't be anything fundamentally wrong with acquiring a few eggs on what was called 'The Black Market', or was there?

I warmed my hands and the settle sheltered my back from the draught of the open door. Then someone scraped his feet on the iron grid on the threshold. "That's Tom," said Mrs Edwards. "How is he today?" asked Mrs Hawkins as she turned to me and explained that Tom had been seriously injured when his tractor had overturned upon him. Tom, a man in his forties, appeared at the door, walked lamely into the room, acknowledged me and joined me on the settle. He then asked how I was settling into my new job. After discussing his illness, I excused myself and made for the door. I left and as the door slammed behind me I wondered what comments were being made about me. I opened the yard gate and retraced my steps through the vicarage grounds.

The moon was silhouetted behind the towering beeches and sycamores in the parkland, and at a lower level homely village lights occasionally revealed themselves and then disappeared. I passed intervening shrubs and bushes where stoats and weasels stalked and killed their evening prey. Piteous cries of suffering punctuated and agitated the night air and then died away, to be followed by other frenzied and tortured screams of animals, suffering the gin-traps until death brought release. I learnt then that nature by night was entirely different from the daytime romantic notion of peace and loveliness expressed by the poets. I was glad to find the relative tranquillity of the village, remote from the fearful and terrified cries of injured creatures, that cried night after night, with their grotesque pleadings unheard. It was only eight o'clock but the village, shrouded by grey mist rising for the river, was stilled except from the pleasant sound of water running free, gurgling and swirling against rocks and groynes overhung by indolent willows and interwoven brambles. This complexity of undergrowth and rocks guided the silver winding stream into dark whirling pools, eroding the banks and sparkling shallows, where the priestly heron fished. Motionless, then cobra-like, she struck with unerring aim and killed, quietly watched by the beady-eyed otter and her three young who slid and practised on the narrow wet slope leading down to the river's edge.

My footsteps echoed on the bridge and attracted the attention of Sam Jones, Maendy, a retired farmer, leaving Miss Parry's with his jug of milk.

"Hello Bowen," he said, and held the door open for me to enter.

"Been for a walk have you?" he asked inquisitively. "Yes," I answered without giving any further information about my proposed purchase of contraband food. He left and Miss Parry, obviously keen to know asked, "Any luck?"

"Three pounds on Thursday," I replied "and two dozen eggs."

"There you are right now," she added. "Come and have some supper before it gets cold." She moved towards the fire where the nimble curling flames licked around the pan, now exuding appetising scents of home-cured bacon.

Mealtimes at Glanyrafon were always delightful occasions when local gossip, accidents, farm sales, world events and some leg-pulling around the lamp-lit room, provided one of our most important social events of the day. Villagers would frequently interrupt and eventually join in our discussions. Then, carrying their milk or butter, they would stumble into the inky darkness outside and wend their lonely ways to one of the local cottages. Through these daily meetings with neighbours on such occasions, in the hay-fields, or at the well, in the shop or inn, people were of greater significance to one another and had a clearer identity than people of more populous areas. Because of the many cross-cutting ties of culture, language, religion and normative values, the local residents were uniquely joined into close communities. Kindred reinforced these ties and, of course, this type of community supported its members in times of duress, bereavement, illness or seasonal activities. It was a vigorous, hard-working community where I never heard anyone speak of depression or admit poverty. A long tradition of peasantry, of animal husbandry, of seeking fuel, of gardening, of religion, of poaching to survive, of servility to the gentry had produced a particular society very different from the urban community where I had my roots. Beulah was in so many ways a tribal society, where families had lived for centuries, under more or less the same social infrastructure.

After a genial meal lively with amusing conversation, blithely unaware of any impending and frightening consequences of my success in acquiring so much Black Market food, I lit the candle and retired to my small bedroom. My bed was iron-framed, with a feather underlay and pillows made from the down feathers of Miss Parry's poultry. On winter nights they radiated such comfort and warmth when one turned and burrowed into the yielding depths. It was Springtime and outside I heard the whistle of the otter living above the bridge, the owl on the spreading sycamore outside, and the haunting cries of more tortured creatures in their death-throes in hedge and wood.

Thursday night's visit to the Vicarage was more or less a repeat of the sequence of events which had taken place on the previous Tuesday when I had made my first rendez-vous with the Vicar's mother, her son and Mrs Edwards. My second visit, however, consolidated our acquaintance. I was offered tea, asked about my parents and much to my surprise discovered that my newly discovered distant cousin was a Member of the Magic Circle. While we were discussing this his mother moved quietly from one room to another, and then appeared with a brown paper bag containing three dozen eggs, each carefully wrapped in newspaper.

"They are very fresh ... they are today's eggs. Watch you don't break them," she said as she carefully handed them to me.

"If you are ready we'll go next door for the butter," she said as she led the way. When we arrived at Aberannell farm, Mrs Edwards, dressed in a floral pinafore, her race ruddy and furrowed with outdoor work, her eyes streaming with cold, received us politely, and deferentially led us into the farmhouse kitchen. The shaggy Welsh collie was abruptly ordered from her vantage-point in front of the coal fire and we were offered the fireside chairs. She excused herself before disappearing into the large larder. While she was away, I took the opportunity of counting the hams and sides of bacon suspended from the painted, wooden ceiling and was amazed to see gutted headless fish, some a foot and a half long, hanging from hooks between the sides of salted bacon.

"What fish are those?" I asked Mrs Hawkins, the Vicar's mother, as I scrutinized the pallid grey bodies, grotesque and stiff.

"Oh, they're smoked salmon," replied Mrs Hawkins, as Mrs Edwards reappeared holding three pounds of butter as yellow as the sun, golden and patterned with oak leaves and acorns.

"There we are," smiled Mrs Edwards, "nine shillings, please. Three shillings a pound is not too much, is it?" she asked.

"No not at all, I'm most grateful to you. Here's the money, can I have some next week?" I asked. "Yes, certainly, I'll keep some for you every week. Come up on Thursday next week and I'll have it ready for you," she said. I thanked them both and almost did a euphoric dance across the kitchen floor. I was intrigued by the fish hanging from the kitchen rafters. If they really were salmon then they were the largest fish I had ever seen, far larger than the rainbow trout I had seen struggling for survival in the polluted Taff at home in Cefn Coed.

"They're beautiful," I said, pointing to the ceiling.

"Oh, they're smoked salmon," replied Mrs Edwards. "The boys catch them in October, when they come up the brooks to spawn and then we smoke them in the chimney. As a matter of fact we give some to the chickens to get them to lay in the spring."

"Unbelievable," I muttered because even tinned salmon was a delicacy in my part of the world. About the only time that a tin of salmon would have been opened in the 'thirties' would have been at a funeral. I was very surprised at the social and cultural differences between rural mid-Wales and the Valleys. It was becoming obvious that I was culturally alienated in the Welsh countryside. This was an entirely different world from that of my occasional romantic excursions, when enjoying the untamed mountain scenery of the Beacons or the lonely lakes and scarred hillsides, gazing onto desolate towns like Merthyr.

"The boys will show you how to catch them in the Autumn," said Mrs Edwards. "How do they catch them?" I asked. "Oh, with a gaff and a torch," she said. I was just as wise because I had no idea what a gaff was. She must have recognized my ignorance and departed into the larder reappearing with a large, bent, barbed iron hook attached to a long rod. "This is a gaff," she said. With that her son Tom appeared and with a look of admonition at his mother, retrieved the gaff and took it back to the larder. I gathered that this instrument was not for public display. Following this silent response from the son and his return to the fireside chair, the conversation became tense and restricted and I was glad to leave. I had somehow intruded into the covert world of poaching, in an area where everyone carried an apparent air of respectability and conformity, hiding the long affray between the poaching peasant and the gentry. I was unaware that for centuries there had been this secret war based upon the need for food, and the feeling on the part of the peasant that fish and game were not the prerogative of the rich. Inadvertently, therefore, I had intruded into the secret world of ancient custom and feelings that transcended laws. Poaching was concerned with survival in obtaining food. During the nineteenth century the penalty, if caught could be transportation for fourteen years, or hanging in the case of sheep-stealing. This was facilitated by the fact that the squires were the local magistrates.

After thanking the ladies, I left and crossed the yard and bridge to the Vicarage parkland. It was wonderful to be released from the constrictive atmosphere of the kitchen and to walk freely on the grass and heavy clay under sycamores new in leaf, sheltering the ewes heavy in lamb. This pastoral hush was again broken by the haunting cries of injured and trapped creatures, pulling and struggling, tearing their flesh to free themselves.

As I unfastened the five-bar gate adjacent to Mrs P's single-storey lodge illuminated by the full moon hanging over Epynt, bright and mysterious, casting shadows broken now by the soft pale glow of the brass paraffin lamp inside the low white-washed dwelling, I glimpsed Mrs P, her grandson and daughter crouching around the hearth with hands outstretched towards the red glow of the coal fire, which spawned the spiral of twisting smoke ascending from the short squat chimney stack. I pondered how she could possibly survive on her weekly pension of a few shillings. She made me aware that one's enthusiasm for the country scene does not take account of the muted pain of rural poverty.

My pessimism, engendered by the brutality of war and rural poverty, was broken as I passed through the village by a female voice calling, "Good-night, Mr Bowen."

"Hello Nurse," I responded to the grey-haired, portly woman who provided about the only bulwark of comfort and succour to the young and old as they entered or departed this cumbrous world.

"How are you?" I asked.

"Tired," she replied.

"I've been up in Abergwesyn all day. A very difficult birth and, unfortunately, although I shouldn't say it, it would be better for this unwanted child to die."

"Why is that, Nurse?" I asked.

"It has no future," she replied.

"Why?" I again asked.

"It's illegitimate, the mother's of low intelligence and given the chance I'm sure, because of her circumstances, she'll kill herself and possibly the child."

"This is awful," I replied. I knew it was not exceptional from my own experience as the son of a nurse who could account for more than one unwanted illegitimate child being allowed to die simply by permitting it to freeze to death or by providing the conditions for pneumonia to develop.

"What are the circumstances, Nurse?" I asked.

"They couldn't be much worse," she replied. "The father of the girl who's had this baby is old, and very unwell. She looks after him."

"What about the father of the baby?" I asked.

"She won't tell us who he is," she added. "Perhaps she doesn't know, anyway."

I acknowledged her confidential information on the matter and bade her good-night as I went towards the bridge over the Camarch leading to Miss Parry's home. I carried my thoughts with me into the warm living room. "Anything wrong?" asked Miss Morgan. "No, not really," I replied, and to change the subject I said, "Come and look at the moon." Both Miss Parry and Miss Morgan slowly crossed the red-tiled floor and peered at the rounded radiation of lunar light, pillowed and marooned in the starry wilderness of the night sky. I couldn't shed my melancholic thoughts, mediated by my reverie of war and then the nurse's story. I couldn't help my outrage when I castigated the earth by saying, "What a world that moon looks upon."

After supper, I sat by the fire and chatted with Miss Parry about her family and her father who had been a waggoner on the Estate. She spoke in reverential tones of a man close to the earth, with a great love of horses with whom he had spent his entire working life. I gazed at her care-worn hands, bruised by toil, and that furrowed face. Her strained, blue eyes bespoke the honesty of peasant stock, caught in the strait- jacket of circumstance which demanded that her natural nobility should bend to the subservience of her class. Her subdued voice and her gentle mien manifested the divinity of women, who toil year in year out as mothers of colliers, wives of brutish men or just rural slaves like Miss Parry. What is the purpose of their lives, if it is only to suffer pain, labour or motherhood, with just an occasional glimmer of recreation or rest? These were early days in the Welsh countryside but I was learning fast. I was beginning to see how people's lives were only a pawn in the game of life. They had little control over the direction or the whole situation of their lives. Theirs was only to suffer the consequences of other people's decisions in war and peace. To be born poor or in a large family of a low wage earner with bright or ignorant parents were crucial determinants in this game of life. How many Miss Parrys have spent and sacrificed their lives in caring for aged parents? I pondered as I left them in the kitchen and climbed the scrubbed staircase to my bedroom sanctuary away from the cares of the world.

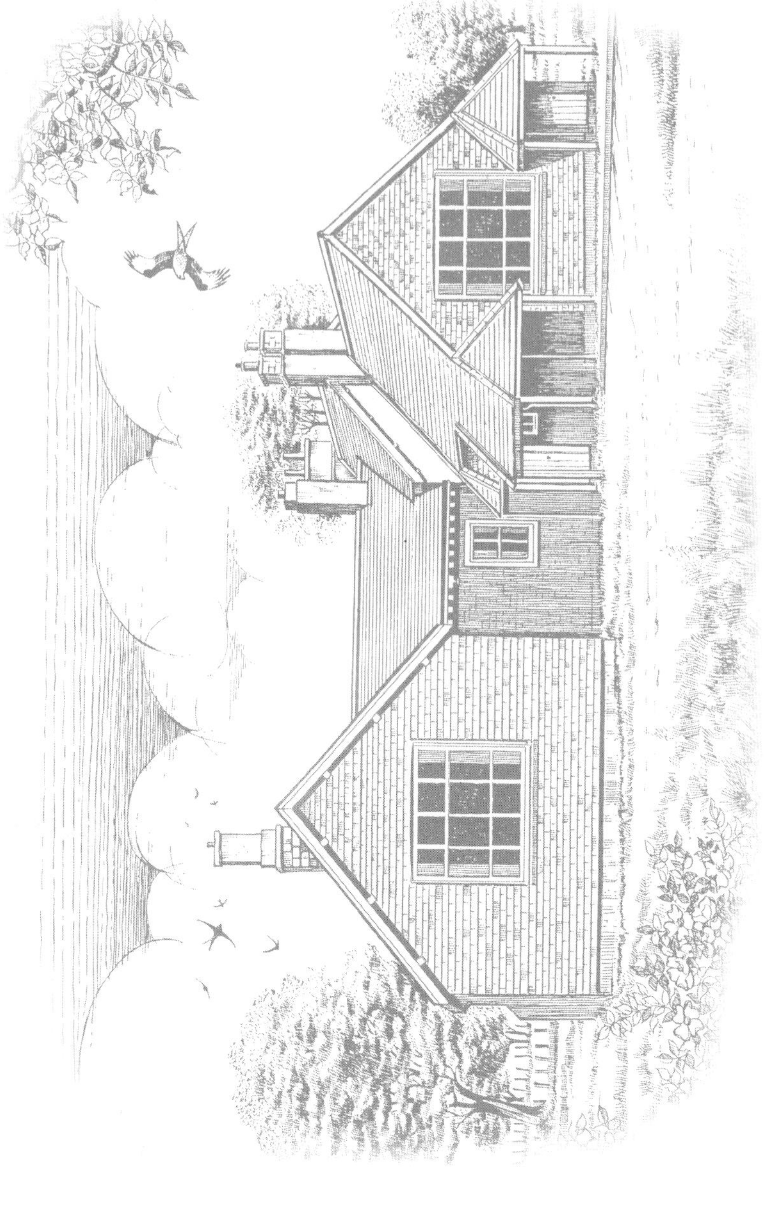

The Food Inspector

MY FIRST FRIDAY AT Beulah was a wonderful day. It was a brilliant Spring day with the air shimmering under an azure sky, totally clear except for some westerly scudding clouds hovering over Llangamarch to the west. The trees fronting the school wore their newest green while the hedges, dressed in darker shades, were alive with bursting buds and sparrows fighting and fluttering among the black branches. A cock pheasant disturbed in a nearby field was protesting raucously as it sped for cover, while the gaping cows paused to look in astonishment at all the bustle, as swooping curlews gliding silently on open wings into the verdant meadows. Insects, light, shadows, birdsong and the sailing sun made this a wondrous time of rural splendour, coloured by varying hues of greenness below the canopy of blue above.

In school the children, boys and girls, buried in earnest endeavour, struggled with furrowed brows, sad eyes thinking and looking pensively into books, or at the ceiling searching for inspiration. Some seemed to be hoping for divine help, or from a neighbour foolish enough to leave his book uncovered, then, having seen the light, busy scribbling to compensate for those lost moments with a smiling countenance relieved of tension, and radiating the pleasure of success. Playtime never came too early when over-energetic boys rolled in the grass, girls skipped while some of the older thirteen and fourteen-year-olds, looked rather scornfully at these childish antics. In July they would be leaving to work on farms in the neighbouring parishes, and entering a life of unending toil broken only by occasional fairs and market days at Builth.

Dinnertime started, while I cooked the dinners. "Cooked" perhaps is an exaggeration, because it involved only three utensils - a black kettle, a saucepan and a frying pan all used for boiling water, frying bacon, boiling eggs or heating tins of beans. I was only seven years older than some of my pupils who yet were so nervous and shy when I spoke to them. However, they were bright, polite and intelligent and worked diligently in school and at the homework which I set them daily. I frequently looked at those lovely faces, red-cheeked and smiling and pondered as to what the future held for them. Alas, Betty Davies and Marina Jones, two delightful little girls, were to die young. After the children had departed at 3.30pm the atmosphere of the school took on a sombre air. One felt the presence of children long gone whose feet had tramped on the floor and whose happy voices had echoed around the classroom walls.

That first Friday afternoon at the school progressed with interminable slowness in spite of what could be described as an indefinable elation associated with the prospect of the week-end break. I departed just after three o'clock, leaving the school and its pupils in the care of Miss Morgan. I strode down the uneven earthen yard under the newly green beech trees and through the lichen-covered gate onto the hollow stretch of road leading to the village. The hedgerows provided a green screen which hid the tractors turning the brown sward, the bleating of lost lambs and the angry shouts of a farmer remonstrating with some over-anxious sheepdog near the village lying in the distance. The green hedge vegetation was relieved by the masses of greater celandines bordering the road, and shadowed by the canopy of willow and hazel catkins overhead. Soon I passed Jim Mathias's smithy where he and Dai Arthur, the wheelwright, were hammering an iron band onto a newly made red wheel.

"Going home for the weekend are you?" shouted Jim as he used his cap to wipe the sweat from his black face.

"Yes," I replied. "It'll be nice to go home for the weekend."

"See you next week then," he shouted. I waved to them and descended the hill leading to the village and the Post Office where I was to catch the bus. First, however, I had to retrieve my butter and eggs from Miss Parry's house. This I did and at the same time called, "Hello, Miss Parry, I'm leaving now. I've got my case, see you Monday." Somewhere in the distance her voice answered, "Right, see you Monday."

With that I closed the door, latched the gate and sped over the bridge in the direction of the Post Office anticipating the bus and a delightful return journey to Cefn Coed. My heart raced at the liberation from this too early responsibility of being a village headmaster at twenty-one years of age. Completely absorbed in these thoughts I stood outside the Post Office waiting for the bus that would take me to Builth on my first lap of the journey home. I glanced at my watch, placed my case carefully on the ground and waited and waited . My repose completely vanished when Mrs Evans, the Post Mistress, opened the door of her cottage office and called out, "Mr Bowen, the bus has gone ten minutes ago."

"It's only twenty-five minutes to four now," I responded.

"Well, it's gone anyway," she added with an assertive nod.

"Thank you, Mrs Evans," I replied and wondered to myself how I was going to cover the fourteen miles to Builth on foot in time to catch the only train home. Until recently it would have been quite in order to 'hook a lift', but my new station in life seemed to suggest that this was an inappropriate action to take. With that a small Morris Eight car appeared round the bend by Bill Cobbler's house, and involuntarily I indicated to the driver that I was in need of a lift. He braked, stopped and before I had reached him he had opened the door. I ran and was greeted by a dark-haired, square- jawed pleasant man with lively blue perceptive eyes.

"Where are you heading for?" he asked.

"I've just missed the bus to Builth," I replied.

"Jump in," he said. "Can I take your case?" he enquired.

He leaned forward to take my case but the weight was such that he struggled for a second and then turned and placed it on the rear seat of the car.

"Get in," he said as he started the engine. I thanked him and immediately he asked me where I was going, what my job was and without turning his head said, "Taking some stuff down for the family are you?"

"Yes," I replied. "I've got three pounds of butter and three dozen eggs in the case and since you've been so kind in giving me a lift would you like a share?"

"No thanks," he politely replied with what appeared to be a faint smile. I felt incredibly happy as I glanced at the sublime beauty of the passing fields, the solemnity of Llanlleonfel church, the grandeur of Garth House and the profusion of white-washed farmsteads and outbuildings. My raptures evaporated when my driver asked, "How long have you been up here?"

"Oh, only a week," I replied.

"Been in the forces have you?" he asked.

"Yes," I replied. "I've just left the army and got this temporary headship up here until I can find a permanent post somewhere."

"I see," he replied as we passed through Garth. After a few minutes he turned to me and said,

"Do you know .... the butcher at ...."

"Yes," I replied, "I know him but have only met him twice."

"Well, he's been fined eighty pounds today for having a pound of butter in with his meat in the fridge".

"Oh, I'm sorry to hear that," I replied.

We sped along and some distance after leaving Garth he turned to me and asked, "Do you know ....?"

"Yes, I know him very well, I see him or his wife every morning".

"Well," he said, "he's been fined £100 today."

"For what?" I innocently asked.

"He claimed that he'd bought a sack of flour to make bread but when I called there and asked if I could see the baking tins he didn't have any and in fact he'd been feeding his pigs with the flour."

"I didn't know they fed pigs on flour," I rather naively stated.

"Yes," he added. "They mix it with potatoes or barley for fattening pigs and it's illegal."

"Oh, I see," I added without fully comprehending exactly.

Suddenly I remembered what he had said, "When I called there and asked for the bread tins." This meant little to me really, but it was fairly obvious, even to a town-dweller, that he held some official position in the rural economy. I circumvented my ignorance by asking him, "Do you work in this area?"

"Yes", he replied. "I'm the Government Food Inspector."

"What does that entail?" I demurely asked.

"My job is to prosecute people breaking the food laws," he said, as he turned and looked at me with an eye that suggested "people like you."

My most immediate reaction to this unpalatable news was a funereal silence, broken only by the throb of the car-engine and my intermittent heartbeat. There were minutes when there was no pulse or breathing. This was a rendez-vous with disaster. What a contrast between these moments and the raptures of an hour before! This sensational news was my swansong. It made me tantamount to being a smuggler carrying contraband my tenure as a Headteacher was going to be extremely limited. I speculated in the long silence as to the amount I would be fined. Three pounds of butter at the current fining rate at Llanwrtyd Court of eighty pounds per pound of butter, amounted to two hundred and forty pounds and three dozen eggs would cost me at least forty pounds a dozen. Another hundred and twenty pounds, total three hundred and sixty pounds! On top of this was the stigma of appearing in court, which would result in losing my job. I shuddered at the possible repercussions - the gossip, the newspaper reports and, of course, I would undoubtedly be asked in court as to where I had procured this Black Market food supply. How was I going to protect the Vicar's mother?

My sheer terror intensified. My total lack of respect for the law, my absurd failure of self-restraint, my incredible stupidity in telling him that I carried this contraband, were incontrovertible evidence of my guilt. There was a grotesque, painful dissonance, discernible by the visible composure of the Food Inspector carefully scrutinizing the frightened creature attempting to appear normal at his side. One astute man exuding confidence and probity, the other the consummation of ineptitude. I was thinking of this terrible opprobrium, this terribly bad luck when he turned to me and said, "How old are you?"

"Twenty-two," I replied. My final degradation came with his next statement. "I'll take you to the station."

I shuddered at this further humiliation, but what did he mean? Was it the Police Station or the Railway Station? How cleverly had he perpetuated my agony. I thought if he slows down at the crossroads in Builth, I could open the door of the car and make a run for it. But then he had my case, I just could not retrieve it from the rear seat before my dash for freedom. In any case, he knew by now who I was. There was no point in it. The only thing that I could do was to attempt to appear brave and normal, and to galvanize what nervous energy that remained prior to my untimely demise at the 'Station'. I buried my suffocating timidity under the shroud of stoical composure. I would plead guilty, claim this to be the first occasion, apologize and pray that the court, understanding my naivety, would give me an admonition and second chance to retrieve my character. I could hardly expect a reprieve from the Chairman of the Education Committee, who as Principal of the Memorial College at Brecon and recently knighted, would probably and rightly feel that they could happily dispense with my services as headmaster.

Reflecting upon this shambles the car stopped outside the Police Station. This is it, I thought. What about a quixotic approach claiming total ignorance of the law? Say that it was a gift and that no payment had been made to my aunt the Vicar's mother. For a moment we gazed into each other's eyes.

"How old did you say you were?" he asked.

"Twenty-two," I deferentially replied.

He reflected for a moment, screwed up his jaw, rubbed it and then suddenly said, "Oh, come on, let's go," as if angry with his own position. Without another word he drove through the town, over the Wye bridge and down to the railway station. He turned, picked up my case and carefully handed it to me. Thanking him, I opened the door and stumbled into the railway station, grateful not to be in the cells of the Police Station, with my contraband confiscated and awaiting trial and disgrace.

The gents' toilet offered a suitable place of retreat from this dangerous world of smuggling butter and eggs. It was there in these uncongenial surroundings that I discovered that I could still breathe, with a fibrillating pulse beating away in my chest. The toot of a whistle indicated the approach of the train. I heard it stop and bolted out from the toilets like a greyhound after a hare. Dismounting from the train was the newly knighted Principal, Sir Joseph Jones, Chairman of the Breconshire Education Committee and Principal of the Memorial College at Brecon. I wondered how I should now address him, but in my confusion and because of my speed and before I really could decide upon the correct title, I hit him in the groin with my case, causing him to double up with pain, and shouted "Sorry, Joe," as I collapsed and tried to hide in a corner seat of the railway carriage. I could see him glaring in anger towards me as I tried to hide my face, praying that he would not recognize me at my next interview for a permanent teaching post in Breconshire. This was a day to remember for ever.

My second encounter with the Food Inspector was in November 1946.

Friday brought my school week to its close and upon reflection, it had been a profoundly interesting week with the stories of the Cannwyll Corff (the corpse candle), freeing the trapped rabbits, and of course for the first time encountering the fish poachers, and having the present of a twelve-pound salmon. Until my pupils arrived at school on the Friday morning, I had forgotten that I had ordered two chickens with one of them. She arrived with a winsome smile, pale, drawn face and ill-fitting thin frock, that hardly kept out the wind and cold which swept over the bleak moorland where she lived in dire rural poverty. On the one occasion I visited her home, I found that the two-part door opened into a single-storey building occupied by two elderly grandparents, a stone-paved floor supporting a round table, upon which a chicken was picking scraps off the top, with a half-grown pig eating and grunting from a bowl underneath. I had seen urban poverty before but this was an entirely new experience about which I had only read.

She was obviously tired by carrying the cardboard box containing the chickens and evidently relieved to place the burden on my desk. I was expecting to see two dead, dressed chickens when I nonchalantly opened the box. Immediately, I fell back under a ferocious onslaught of claws and feathers, as I was attacked by these demoniac fighting cockerels. They flew with talons outstretched, wings outspread, rapacious and unrelenting in their attack, so that I retreated with blood dripping from my chin and gladly closed the classroom door upon them.

No children could enter, no lessons could be taught unless I found some way of capturing these brutes. Here was another aspect of rural life that came as a shock, since I had never been subjected to such a vicious attack by any creature previously. They were obviously of the same breed, red-feathered, with blood-red hackles, thick- legged, yellow-beaked, with black evil eyes. These proud kings of the farmyard were now pompously strutting and pecking at the wooden floor, seeking any challenge to their power. I kept them under surveillance for some minutes and galvanizing my strength, worked out a plan of counter-attack upon them.

I dressed up in my flying clothes, leather coat, helmet, gauntlets and goggles used now for motor cycling on my new 500cc AJS. I found a sack and spotted a shepherd's crook in the corner of the middle classroom. What I had to do was avoid if possible a simultaneous assault, so that when I eventually dived into the attack, I took the nearest by surprise, caught him by the throat and amidst cries of fiendish anger, and flying feathers, bundled him into the sack. As the other monster rallied for another onslaught, I temporarily stunned him with a swing of the crook. In a second, he too was shoved, clawing, pecking and fighting, into the mouth of the sack. Within the confines of the sack they fought a violent and bloody battle. Exhausted by fear and anger, I tied the neck of the sack and left them to battle it out in the porch with my motorcycle, my bag of salmon, eggs and butter some distance away from them.

The children duly arrived from distant farms soaked in the

torrential rain, and our first job was to remove wet stockings, coats and shoes and arrange them round the guards of the large tortoiseshell stoves. Until transport was laid on for them, some were walking over two miles to school, while those from Cwm Cyn Nos walked over open moorland paths strewn with glass to guide them to the nearest road between Beulah and Abergwesyn. On stormy days they arrived red-faced, bright-eyed with trembling raindrops falling from caps and hoods. They clustered round the fires, warming their hands and in turn drying their heads, so that their hair sprouted into dishevelled tufts and curls. Outside the rain lashed against the windows, driven by wild winds howling through the trees and leafless hedges, under which cows and sheep cowered in hopeless resignation. There were days in the mountains when nature became uncontrollable and untameable, when the shaggy hills and sombre stretches of fields and hedges and the subtle beauties of the countryside were hidden in mist and rain.

Occasionally, during the morning I visited the porch and found that the sack and cockerels had moved a few feet one way or another, stopping against a wall or bench, as they continued their battle. Dinnertime came and, using my kettle, frying pan and saucepan I was able to cook or boil the various items of bacon, eggs or beans which the farm children had brought to school. I closed school a little earlier than usual because the storm showed no sign of abatement, as black clouds moved like a great tent over the sodden earth. After warning the children of the dangers of flooded streams and slippery foot bridges, and the importance of arriving home before dark, I sent them home early, into the cascading rain and approaching twilight.

I immediately dressed for my homeward journey over the deserted, farmless Epynt mountain, used now by the military authorities as a gun range. Wearing a macabre array of flying coat, leather helmet, goggles, wellingtons and gauntlets, I threw the bag of butter and eggs over my back; the salmon was across my chest supported underneath by my belt, while the cockerels and sack were placed in a cardboard box tied securely to my rear seat.

After bidding farewell to Mrs Evans, Cilderwen, my caretaker, I wove through the flooded road to Garth and climbed the northern flank of the Epynt, carefully avoiding the unfenced earthen kerb on my left which served as the only barrier between the road and a sheer drop of hundreds of feet into Cwm Graig Ddu.

As I reached the summit, I met the full force of the south-westerly storm. The raindrops stung my face and the wind came in sudden bursts casting me across the road, spattered with pools which glistened in my wavering headlight. The wind played a requiem in the skies over this dreary inhospitable tract of melancholy moorland. Fortunately, I was familiar with the turns and falls of this hostile environment, and then I approached the deserted Drovers' Arms. Suddenly, I felt some ominous bumps coming from my rear wheel. I knew immediately that I had a flat tyre and, to make matters worse, no pump. I pulled in slowly to the side, confirmed my suspicions and wondered whether to walk back to Garth, some six miles back, or walk forward to Upper Chapel, which had a pub and a farmhouse about the same distance away. I really was in dead trouble.

Fortunately, I was not entirely in an alien environment, because I was regularly travelling over this road and had explored the Drovers' Arms in daylight. The previous year I had found a cock grouse rising in a flurry of red feathers and an eerie cry from some rushes behind the inn, where I later found a nest with twenty eggs. The only shelter available to me now was the rear doorway bolted and securely held by padlocks. I cowered for two hours against the stout door, cold, hungry, angry to such an extent that I finally decided to walk to Upper Chapel through the driving storm. As I emerged from the shelter of the inn doorway, the surrounding hills were revealed by unexpected flashes of lightning, followed by resounding thuds of thunder echoing through the deserted valleys. South of me, however, a headlight appeared lighting up the sky before vanishing and then re-appearing nearer and nearer. This was a vehicle of some sort heading from the south in my direction which I hoped would save me from this wretched wilderness of pre-historic cairns, where Neolithic ghosts screamed mournfully from the dark hollows and bogs around me.

I stood counterpoised against the storm in the middle of the road, as the beam of light ultimately glared into my eyes. My spectral presence brought the small car to a halt. I moved towards the driver and shouted to him through the narrow gap of the side window, "I've got a puncture. Can you lend me a pump please?"

"Yes," he replied as he lowered his head and opened the boot of the car.

"Thank you," I replied and now, with his headlights full on me, I pumped away at my rear wheel. When it felt hard I undid the pump, rushed over to him thanked him and was returning to my motorcycle when I heard him shout.

"Hey, by the way, are you the schoolmaster from Beulah?"

"Yes," I replied.

"What have you got with you tonight?" he asked.

"A salmon, two chickens, three pounds of butter and three dozen eggs," I answered in an angry and defiant mood, exacerbated by my frozen clothes and hunger. We both felt aware of the situation. I had abandoned all respect for his status as a Food Inspector and there was no way that he was going to take me into his car and humiliate and taunt me as he had done previously. My feelings of contempt and repugnance grew stronger as I stood defiantly in his headlights. He remained silently contemplating what his next move should be when a hearse approached carrying a coffin. I knew that the coffin was full of Black Market butter and was smiling to myself when the driver suddenly shouted, "All right, Mr Bowen?" "Yes," I replied and with that the Food Inspector shouted, " I hope I never see you again." As I leapt on my bike I retorted, " I hope I never see you again either."

I arrived home at Cefn Coed about ten o'clock to find my family beside themselves in great distress, because I was five hours late. They had come to the conclusion that I was probably lying dead or injured somewhere along my fifty-eight mile route over the Brecon Beacons and Mynydd Epynt. The police had been contacted and plans were afoot to search for me. However, they were overjoyed to see me and the search was called off and the police were not told anything about my encounter with the Food Inspector. My father released the cockerels into our pen of chickens at the top of the garden and then proceeded to clean the cock salmon. Because it was out of season the flesh was white, and such a rare delicacy that it was decided to give it to a local lad who had broken his back and become paralyzed. Both cockerels ended their days rather ingloriously: one was shot for killing a cockerel on a neighbouring farm while the other, which had been sold to the cemetery sexton, was likewise shot for violently attacking funeral mourners. Many tombstones still bear testimony to the many abortive attempts made by the sexton to shoot this vicious bird with his 303 Home Guard rifle!

A Community in Change

I DISCOVERED THAT THE VILLAGE of Beulah was situated some four miles from Llanwrtyd and fourteen from Builth in the Irfon Valley. To the north was the rugged upland region of Abergwesyn, and to the south Llangamarch, lying in the shadow of the northern flank of the Epynt mountain range. The Spa towns of Builth, Llandrindod, Llangamarch and Llanwrtyd had enjoyed considerable popularity from the coming of the railway era in the mid-nineteenth century until the early decades of this century.

In 1945 Beulah comprised, as previously mentioned, around twenty cottages tied to the Llwyn Madoc Estate, a Post Office, an inn, a school, a wheelwright's shop, a blacksmith, a vicarage, a village hall, a Nonconformist chapel, a shoemaker's shop, a carpenter's shop, a district nurse's residence and two shops. About half a mile north of the village was Eglwys Oen Duw, Llwyn Madoc House, the mock-Tudor mansion home of the squire, Commander Evan Thomas, a disused corn mill, Dolaeron woollen mill now converted to a dwelling-house and the home farm occupied by Mr Lamacroft, the estate agent or steward. The Estate had been owned by the Thomas family for generations, and its many scattered farms straddled the three neighbouring parishes. The Estate farms were serviced by a staff of masons and carpenters who lived in the tied cottages. Many of these cottagers had three acres of land which supported one cow, a pig and some chickens. Some of the cottagers sold milk and made three or four pounds of butter weekly, some of which was sold in order to supplement the meagre old age pensions of around ten shillings a week for those over seventy. The cottage rental was around two shillings and sixpence a week, paid twice yearly. The farms varied in size from smallholdings to farms of 50-100 acres, and were stocked with sheep, cattle, pigs and poultry. Rents of the Estate farms were paid half-yearly at Llwyn Madoc.

Writing of Llwyn Madoc mansion in 1926, Herbert Vaughan,

a member of the gentry class himself, described it thus: "What a charming peaceful spot was Llwyn Madoc nestling in a fold of the narrow valley of the Cammarch, midway between Garth and Abergwesyn, amid the wildest scenery. The long low rambling house, set off by a succession of brilliant flower beds in lawns of velvet smoothness, made a veritable human oasis amidst the solemn woods and moors and swelling hills."

Until recently, like most rural communities, the district was largely self-sufficient and rarely was it necessary for the countryman to leave his locality for the necessities of life. Most rural dwellers lived and died in intimate co-existence. Most of the food required by the community was grown locally and from the animals they had meat, skins, wool and milk. Ironwork was made by the smith, furniture by the carpenters, carts by the wheelwrights, cloth by the weavers, flour by the miller, shoes by the shoemaker and Beulah could also boast a pig-killer (Dafydd Lewis, Pencae) and gamekeepers who reared pheasants and controlled foxes, stoats, polecats and birds of prey. Nurse Lewis was the local midwife and nurse.

Crucial to the rural economy was the co-operation between farmers, craftsmen and cottagers, especially at times of high seasonal activity, such as hay-making or shearing. Cottagers were recompensed for days spent in the farmers' hayfields by being permitted to grow a few rows of potatoes with a load of manure or a sack of swedes given in return for their labour. Local custom determined which of his neighbours a farmer co-operated with and when a farm changed hands the newcomer usually accepted the same partners as his predecessor in his work group. Shearing and harvesting were important events in the agricultural and social life of the locality. Shearing day was usually held on the same day for each individual farm from year to year and brought together members of the 'work group' and relatives. On the shearing day farmers and servants sat at the same table and there were no social distinctions, but the economic status of the farmer was reflected in the quality of his shearing feast. Hospitality and generosity were pre-eminent among the traditional values and were determinants of local status. These co-operative activities were very important social events to a scattered farming community. When the evening shearing feast was over and tools put away, the people gathered round the hearth and gossiped, reminisced, discussed market prices and when all time-honoured topics had been fully reviewed, returned to their lonely farmsteads.

Farmers and cottagers occasionally bought fresh meat, but invariably the meat supply was derived from the pig, either their own or that shared with family or neighbours at pig-killing time. Salt bacon was a basic meal once or twice every day and therefore the physical development of the pig was a source of interest and concern because of its dietary importance, and also because it involved a relatively considerable financial investment. Pig-killing day was literally and metaphorically a 'big day', commencing early with the lighting of the boiler to provide hot water. From the different parts of the carcase several meat foods were prepared, namely faggots, chitterlings, brawn, lard and scratchlings. Lard mixed with soot was used as a form of water proofing for boots, while I witnessed my landlady, Miss Esther Parry, Glanyrafon, using the thin transparent membrane found over the lard for cuts and abrasions. In my childhood the pig's bladder was used as a football by the boys of Cefn Coed.

Miss Parry, with whom I lodged for six years after a brief period at Wylfa, practised a peasant economy based on her three acres of land, her cow, pig and chickens. She sold milk daily to regular clients who were also villagers. From the surplus milk she made three or four pounds of butter weekly which she also sold to her milk customers. The eggs she sold daily and some were kept for her domestic needs of frying or boiling or for making cake or tart. Bacon provided breakfast, dinner and sometimes supper, with a small portion of meat purchased from the travelling butcher, Mr Jones of Llanwrtyd, who called on Thursday night. The arrival of Mr Jones was always an excuse to obtain news in return for a cup of tea and a Welsh cake. When Dai Pencae killed her pig she followed the custom of giving parts to family and friends. They likewise reciprocated and thus there was a system of 'mutual aid' within the community which extended to the loan of implements among farmers and their family and friends. Her garden provided most of the vegetables and all the potatoes which she required for the winter. With her two fields, which adequately produced sufficient pasture and hay for her Jersey cow, she was almost self-sufficient in terms of food supplies. The money derived from her small pension and the sale of milk, butter and eggs, paid for clothes, shoes, coal and other requirements, which were few. Her survival depended entirely upon buying only the absolute necessities. Shoes or rather nailed boots were repaired by Bill Jones the shoemaker, until they fell apart. Likewise clothes worn in manual work were patched and repaired regularly. Frequently, people used washed sacks over their shoulders in wet and cold weather. Sunday, however, saw chapel and churchgoers wearing their best clothes, as they did in funerals which were attended only by men.

Within this community the family was the primary social group and the unit of economic production. Very few farms employed either male or female labour, all the farmwork being done by members of the family. One of the exceptions was at Maesllech, a farm owned by Mr and Mrs Elvet Powell, who employed two male and one female servant. Of the two men, the older was regarded as a gwas fferm, a farm servant who was unmarried and lived in, while the farm labourer was the son of a cottager. The farm servant became a farm labourer upon marriage, and henceforth accepted a different contract. Although servants often ate in the back kitchen and not at their employers' table, they were usually regarded as members of the family. They were expected to work from seven o'clock in the morning, usually until around seven to eight in the evening. It was generally a 'give and take' arrangement with time off for fairs, funerals and weddings and no loss of wages at times of illness.

I gathered that Miss Parry's father had been a waggoner on the estate and was regarded by tradition as the aristocrat among the servants. This status was derived from the tradition that the horse was the most noble animal in European and Celtic tradition. The groom was a prominent member of the king's court, and only rarely according to the Welsh Laws were horses put to the plough. As the Laws state, "Neither horses, mares nor cows are to be put to the plough." By 1945 these specialized workers such as waggoners, cowmen and shepherds had ceased to exist, but there was a communal shepherd who was paid annually by a group of farmers for attending to the sheep on the hill. The tendency was to hire a man for general farmwork.

There was a fairly clear division of labour between men and women. Female labour was largely confined to the house and farmyard. The mistress was responsible for making butter, she cared for the poultry, assisted with milking and haymaking and largely obtained her housekeeping money from her 'basket money', i.e. the sale of butter and eggs etc. Farmers' sons and daughters worked for their keep, receiving money for clothes or pocket money at irregular intervals. Marriage brought a change of status with the father helping his son to set up a farm with stock and implements, the bride's family providing bedding, furniture and kitchen utensils. There were of course variations according to circumstances. It was apparent that brides with the experience and background of farming were preferred as spouses for farmers' sons. It was governed, too, by economic considerations and it was also important to marry someone of comparable status.

In a community where most people were born locally, the cross-cutting ties of kinship were important. I found that it was of far greater significance than in urban communities. Kinship was a force to be reckoned with, as many a clergyman or schoolmaster has found to his cost. It affected every sphere of social life from neighbourliness to marriage alliances. Bound up with kinship were regulations controlled by sanctions imposed upon family offenders. The strength of kinship was made manifest on occasions such as times of illness or death, and attendance at funerals. Prior to the use of hearses, the dead were often carried a long distance from some upland farms to the graveyard by family and friends.

Water for domestic use was obtained from the village well situated at the side of the main road at Beulah and undoubtedly highly contaminated. A daily scene, therefore, was of men and women carrying buckets of water from the roadside well. Water required for the cows or pigs was taken from the river. Light was provided by an Aladdin's lamp fuelled by paraffin bought at one or other of the village shops. Miss Parry and most other families had Aladdin lamps which provided a reasonable degree of illumination for reading. Outside lanterns were used both on the farms and by cottagers. Houses varied considerably both in size, age, plan and constructional materials. The oldest appeared to be attached cottages having virtually identical plans to urban ironworkers' cottages in the industrialized areas of Wales, while the modern estate houses like Miss Parry's were of red brick with a ground floor plan of large kitchen or living room, a large back kitchen with a long white scrubbed table, two benches, one of which was used for pig-killing, a tin bath, milk separator used for removing cream for butter-making and a traditional butter churn. In addition, there was a large pantry and a small parlour which housed treasured family photographs and the best furniture. The Welsh dresser of local craftsmanship in the living room was used for what it was intended for and not as a piece of antique furniture holding expensive plates and jugs. Upstairs there were three bedrooms, iron bedsteads with feather beds and pillows, rag mats and the papered walls decorated with framed pictures carrying Biblical quotations such as, "Carry ye one another's burdens."

In general, then, the large living room was the centre of family life, and the layout of the kitchen was dominated by the elaborate fireplace, with its 'oven and sham.' On the one side was an iron oven and on the other a boiler with the tops serving as hobs. There was a chain hanging from the chimney on which the black kettle was always hung. The high shelf supported ten brass candlesticks with a china dog in the middle. On either side of the fireplace were armchairs which were always proffered as a token of hospitality to any visitors, prior to their being offered a meal on the bwrdd mawr. There was no loitering after the meal was over, and everyone was urged to move to the fireside, to the aelwyd (hearth) which was the ancient focus around which the Welsh family has gathered over the centuries to converse.

All the farmsteads showed, with few exceptions, a marked preference for a southerly or south-easterly aspect, with the living room facing south and the slate benched dairy with small window facing north or north-west. The choice of farmstead sites was influenced by the need for shelter and a convenient water-supply. The layouts varied greatly from site to site, with the farmhouse and principal buildings either attached or detached. The main outdoor buildings on an average-sized farm comprised the cowhouse, stable, hay barn, carthouse, pigsties, poultry sheds and sometimes a tractor shed and a garage.

There was very little overt evidence of social distinctions at Beulah in 1945. The squire belonged to the gentry class and the land agent was a buffer between him and the tenants of his estate who had a common cultural and educational background. There was some considerable distinction between the independent farmer who owned a well-stocked farm of over a hundred acres, and a wage-earner with a cottage and a few rented fields. The possession of wealth and its reflection in terms of material possessions, levels of education, style of life, quality and size of household and number of servants indicated social status and prestige. Craftsmen and tradesmen occupied an intermediate position between the farmers and cottagers and to these classes may be added the group of professionals such as the clergy, ministers and teachers, who provided specialized services. They carried the prestige associated with their offices and standards of education. There was free social contact between all classes and groups except with the local gentry family. Class distinctions, however, expressed themselves above all in family marriage preferences. Non-economic factors played a part in social status, too, such as having native ability, being a recognized poet, having qualities of generosity or helpfulness, or by holding a position such as magistrate. There was little of the old political alignment of Church-Tory versus Nonconformist-Radical visible in local life. I was appointed head of the village Non-Provided School, my assistant was a Nonconformist, while my caretaker was also the Church caretaker. There was a liberal acceptance of people according to their worth; political affinity was unknown.

Without fully realizing it then in 1945, I was privileged to witness and be part for a brief period of a culture that was dramatically changing from an economy primarily involved and concerned with producing the essential requirements of a rural community, rooted in antiquity, custom and tradition to one depending upon the sale of some local products and the purchase of goods produced elsewhere. After the setting up of the Milk Marketing Board in 1932 local farmers sold their milk daily, for which they received a regular monthly cheque. This sale of milk resulted in the decline of local butter-and cheese-making. Both items could now be purchased in the village shop instead of from the village farm. During this century both the corn mill and woollen mill at Beulah had closed. Flour was purchased for domestic cooking from the village shops, while barley meal for pigs was obtained from the agricultural suppliers at nearby Garth. Woollen goods were obtainable either from the Cambrian Woollen mill at Llanwrtyd, or from the shops at Builth. Within a decade of my arrival at Beulah in 1945, the shoemaker, blacksmith and wheelwright had closed their workshops forever and an essential element in the rural economy contributing to self-sufficiency had disappeared. Today, pig-killing has ended and with it has gone the itinerant pig-killer, the last of whom was Dai Lewis of Pencae. There is no longer an exchange of meat among friends and neighbours; instead, meat is now bought entirely from the town butchers. Professional shearers now move from one farm to another and haymaking has changed to machinists who cut and bag the hay in circular plastic bags. The close co-operation between farmers, craftsmen and cottagers has thus ended and with it have disappeared the cohesive social functions of rural life. Co-operation has been replaced by competition, the horse by the tractor, the gambo by tractor-drawn trailer and the wooden wheel by the pneumatic tyre.

With these crucial changes in the rural economy, farmers have found it necessary to keep accurate accounts and to suffer the trauma of European regulations with regard to milk quotas, subsidies, and so on. With social change old customs such as gwlana, whereby cottagers were permitted to collect wool from the fences and hedgerows, for the spinning of yarn and the labour barter system, have gone. New technology has transformed farming and high interest rates have made it a financial nightmare, exacerbated by low prices for livestock and wool. Non-economic factors such as the family bonds of kinship, membership of church or chapel and strong affinity with neighbours and locality tend to tie people to a particular locality but depopulation of the Welsh countryside continues to deprive these areas of many of their most intelligent young people, who, in so many cases, would be the natural leaders of their communities.

Poets, Dogs and Shepherds

MY FIRST SUMMER TERM at Beulah was taken up with trying to adjust to a rural culture and to organize a school of about forty pupils, whose ages ranged from five to fourteen, and assisted by my supplementary teacher, Miss Morgan. One of my primary tasks that summer was the requisition for the following year. My annual allowance was fourteen pounds. This was expected to cover textbooks, exercise books and equipment. My salary at this time was about eighteen pounds a month, about five pounds more than I had been earning as a physical education teacher at home. There were moments when I wondered why I had taken up this post in such a remote area. I was fourteen miles from Builth and my only mode of transport was a bicycle. In the evenings I went on long treks into the countryside, starting about 4.15pm and lasting until I returned around 9.00pm. On one of these trips to Abergwesyn I saw Llwyn Madoc house for the first time. This had been the home of the Thomas family for generations. It was built into the wooded eastern flank of the valley, a mile north of the village, and its size and grandeur with its brick-walled garden, lawns and lake represented the distinction of social class between the occupants, the squire, Commander Evan Thomas, and his tenants.

Just north of Llwyn Madoc was the old corn mill, Melin y Cwm, now disused and used for storing timber. This was a typical estate mill, where for centuries tenants had been compelled by local laws to have their corn ground and where annually the local peasantry had to fulfil ancient obligations known as 'suit of mill.' This entailed clearing the water leats to and from the mill and carrying wood to repair the mill and so on. This was the centre from which the estate workers, carpenters and masons daily received their orders, made gates and barn doors. The road wove and climbed among steep-sided hill-farms and bare-topped hills, to the almost deserted hamlet of Abergwesyn with its one shop and Post Office and the closed Grouse Inn, closed school and church. This hamlet once echoed and re-echoed to the lowing of herds of cattle, moving at the rate of a few miles a day, controlled by the cattle drovers, some mounted on sturdy ponies and accompanied by their corgis. The cattle wended their way along Cefn Cardis road at Beulah, on to Llanafan Fawr and then to the English fairs where they were later fattened on lush meadows. This route to the English markets had been established centuries ago, with blacksmiths' shops along the way to shoe the cattle when their shoes had fallen off. It was here, too, that the famous hymn writer William Williams of Pantycelyn had served as a curate prior to his being refused ordination in the Church of England, by his vicar, the famous Theophilus Evans, in 1743. Williams later became Wales' greatest hymn-writer, a highly talented poet and one of the leaders of the Methodist Revival.

Another summer's forage into the nearby countryside took me to Llanafan Fawr where I met Dick Swann the headmaster. He had served here after his discharge from the army in the First World War, when he had been captured by the Turks at Kut el Amara. This was the longest siege in British military history, when the surrounded British soldiers were reduced to eating grass to survive. By a very strange coincidence my father had fought with the 24th South Wales Borderers in the relief of Kut el Amara. This knowledge established a close friendship between myself and this former commissioned officer who had sought and found peace in this remote hamlet in mid- Wales. He frequently showed me his private collection of war medals, which he claimed was the best in Wales.

At Glandulais, half-way between Beulah and Llanafan Fawr, was the famous Troedrhiwdalar Congregational Chapel, noted for its famous minister, David Williams (1779-1874) who was minister here for 71 years (i.e. from 1803 until his death) and also for the fact that Dafydd Jones, a drover from Caeo, was converted here and became a well-known hymn-writer and translator. Jim Mathias, the Beulah blacksmith, had his other smithy here, where he worked two days a week. I frequently walked to the neighbouring village of Garth or past the Roman fort at Caerau farm on my way to Llangamarch famous for its barium wells. It was also the birthplace of John Penry (1563-93), the martyr born at Cefnbrith, and the last resting place in the little church yard of the Reverend Theophilus Evans who lived at Llwyn Einon, Llangamarch, and was a noted historian in his day. His most celebrated work was Drych y Prif Oesoedd (1716). His grandson, Theophilus Jones, who lies in the same grave at Llangamarch, wrote one of the most complete county histories, The History of Brecknock, in 1805.

The Reverend Theophilus Evans of Llangamarch stated that a severe attack of scurvy was cured by his drinking the waters of the 'stinking well' at Llanwrtyd and so the claim has been made that it was he who discovered the wells at Llanwrtyd, containing such elements as potassium, sodium, magnesium, calcium and sulphurated hydrogen. With the expansion of the railways in the last century, Llanwrtyd developed as a popular spa and holiday resort for those seeking fresh air, good food and country sports. In 1945 I found Llanwrtyd with its shops, inns, banks and hotels to be the commercial centre for the villages of the upper Irfon Valley. Soon I became acquainted with two if its well-known characters, Jim Jones the Shop and Danny Davies, a teacher at the Llanwrtyd Primary School. Danny lived at Bryn Irfon hotel, built by his industrious father, a local blacksmith, at the turn of the century. Monotony was relieved during my first term at Beulah by frequent trips with Danny in his Austin Seven to Llandrindod. I drove without L plates and, theoretically at least, was covered by my motorcycle licence which I purchased in June 1945.

Life in Beulah and some sixty miles from my home at Cefn Coed was very restricted without some form of motorized transport. Prior to purchasing my motorcycle and with sixty pounds given me by my mother, I set out one evening to purchase a car at the Black Lion garage at Builth, fourteen miles away. The garage owner offered me a small pre-World War II Austin for sixty five pounds but my resources were unfortunately limited to sixty pounds and he just would not reduce the price. I reluctantly and miserably had to cycle another fourteen miles back to Beulah. As I approached Cilmeri a grey Rover stopped and Mr Emrys Evans, Director of Education for Breconshire, emerged.

"Hello, Mr Bowen," he said. "How are you settling down?" After some exchanges he said, "I'll call and see you next week," and with that he sped away towards Builth leaving me to continue my journey to Beulah.

I was busy cooking the school dinners for my forty charges on the following Wednesday when Mr Emrys Evans and the School Attendance Officer arrived. The aroma of home-cured bacon, fried eggs, cocoa and sandwiches permeated the schoolroom as children, red-faced and innocent, chatted happily unaware of the problems of the post-war period, or of the importance of the white-haired Director of Education standing in front of them.

"I'll tell you why we've come, Mr Bowen," he said. "It's to seek directions to the home of the poet, David Lewis of Pencae."

I gave him the necessary instructions and pointed out to him that it entailed a long walk from Pantycelyn Chapel, over very rough moorland, to a remote valley called Cwm Cyn Nos (Valley before Night). It was thus called because local legend stated that unless you got out of the valley before night, then you would fail to do so.

Some days later they returned and informed me that they had found the home of David Lewis and confirmed his brilliance as a poet, by stating that they had given him a topic for an englyn as he started to plough a furrow in one of his fields, and by the time he returned, he had completed the poem following the strict rules of this form of poetry. I met Mr Lewis for the first time some weeks later on the bridge at Beulah and enquired whether I could borrow a Welsh dictionary from him. He informed me that he had six, and that if I came up to Pencae, he would present me with one. Unfortunately, within minutes of our meeting he died at his sister's house. Upon hearing this news, I decided to go on a pilgrimage to his remote homestead in Cwm Cyn Nos as soon as possible.

The opportunity to visit Pencae came the following week, when at four o'clock on the Tuesday, I set forth for Abergwesyn. I arrived at the Williams Pantycelyn Chapel in an hour and then trudged over the rough moorland track to Cwm Cyn Nos. This deep, isolated, green valley with a few small enclosed fields, contrasted sharply with the lunar landscape totally bereft of tress or shelter of any kind whatsoever. Two white-washed single-storey dwellings stood out, one on my left, and the other on the distant side of the valley. This suggested that one or other was the home of the late poet, David Lewis.

Pencae was a quaint, stone-built building, with a slated roof and a door set in the middle of the front elevation with small windows on each side. I looked through the first window into a small kitchen. The opposite wall was lined with books. Outside was a small courtyard surrounded by a low wall and paved with cobble-stones. Nearby was another simple dwelling of exactly the same proportions, and in this case the ascending column of smoke indicated someone in residence. I knocked lightly on the roughly painted door. It was opened by a short, red-faced, blue-eyed smiling woman in her seventies. She had hardly commenced to address me in Welsh, when four of the largest, most vicious dogs threw themselves upon me from the sides of her billowing black skirt. I retreated before this onslaught, kicking and flailing my arms and stick as I attempted to keep them from tearing my body to shreds. With that, the old lady re-appeared, armed with a thick hazel rod with which she thrashed the dogs and bombarded them with invectives and threats. They yelped, cowered and crawled, tails between their legs, into the living room. She apologized, and beckoned me to follow her into the low-ceilinged room.

I nervously followed her, expecting at any moment that one of these monsters would throw itself upon me again. Here they were, the four of them, one lying in front of the fireplace, another under a chair, one to my left and another under the table. Deep-throated growls came from the shadows and when I had eye-contact with the black-and-white brute under the chair, it bared its fangs as a warning, instinctively indicating its total dislike of strangers. I was offered a seat by this lady next to the white scrubbed deal table, under which lay one of the dogs. I sat down expecting to have my legs bitten at any moment. She detected my apprehension and then sent them all crouching fearfully to the earthen floor, with another screaming outburst in Welsh. These sulking, clearly ferocious creatures were obviously terrified of her and one or two emitted a kind of fearful and submissive whimpering cry, as they withdrew further from her. She asked me in Welsh whether I would have a glass of milk, and disappeared into a rear room that might have served as a larder. As far as I could ascertain, the plan of this cottage resembled the ground floor of an ironworker's cottage, with the front door opening into a large living room, with access to two small rooms on the right. I presumed that one was a larder and the other a bedroom. This assumption, however, must have been incorrect, because she later informed me that she had reared six sons and a daughter in this small dwelling. Where had this family of father, mother and seven children slept?

In the course of our conversation I discovered that she had taught her children to read in Welsh, using the Welsh Bible as a textbook. The reason for her teaching the children to read was that they were unable to get to school due to the distance from Cwm Cyn Nos to the main Beulah to Abergwesyn road. From this point on the road near Pantycelyn Chapel they would still have had about three miles to walk to Beulah School. In the wintertime, the children would have been walking over rugged moorland in the dark both ways. She further informed me that now her grown-up sons worked on farms in and around the Elan Valley, except her son Dai, the pig-killer, who lodged with his aunt at Beulah when not at home with her. Her sons walked up to ten miles each day from these distant farms to spend Sundays with her. None of her children had married; her daughter had intended to marry but had changed her mind at the last moment. I was very surprised to see a container of Calor Gas in her living room, and when I mentioned this, she informed me that her sons had carried this and her organ over the moorland to her home.

Her son, known locally as Dai Pencae, had been a man of about fifty years of age, tall, lean but muscular, sharp-eyed and invariably dressed in rough Welsh tweeds and a battered brown trilby that undoubtedly afforded some shelter and protection from the biting winds which swept the rugged landscape of Abergwesyn. His shoulders in winter were usually covered by a washed hempen sack, tied by a pin under his stubbled chin.

In this remote upland valley denuded of trees and shelter the domestic fuel was peat, cut from the nearby hilltops in June and July. It was then left to dry for some days and stored for the winter. Somehow these hill people wrested a sparse living from these smallholdings of a few fields, some sheep and a few cows which provided milk and butter, which together with the eggs gave them a small income. Seeking a living here with a short growing season, harsh climate, a grudging soil and heavy rainfall provided a lonely and precarious livelihood. It nevertheless produced a hardy breed of people given to poetry, religion, music and scholarship. Through hardship and sacrifice these hardworking people strove in endless toil and precariously existed on the verge of starvation. This was especially so when the harvest failed, or stock died, or when the father or mother was struck down with illness. Somehow some contrived to send their sons and daughters to the local Grammar Schools and then to Universities. This is the background of so many of Wales's most eminent sons and daughters; children of the farms and smallholdings. At this time in 1945 the school at Abergwesyn had closed because of rural depopulation and local farm children were now conveyed daily by car to the school at Llanwrtyd, and when older by bus to Builth Secondary School.

The resounding and disturbing ring of horses' hoofs on the road by night at Beulah was a sure sign of a medical problem somewhere in the local countryside. The destination for the night rider was invariably Nurse Davies's house. She would then follow on by walking to some isolated hill farm to deliver a baby, or attend to the sick. During my stay at Beulah from 1945 until I was appointed Headmaster of Penderyn C.P. School in 1951, there was an annual auction held at Beulah for the Nursing Association when all the farmers round about donated some sheep. On one occasion, while innocently attending this unique sale, held outside the Reading Room, I found, much to my surprise, that three sheep were knocked down to me by the auctioneer, I protested that I had not indicated in any way that I wanted to purchase them, that I had nowhere to keep them, and that I knew nothing about sheep, but to no avail. I pleaded with my friend, Elvet Powell, to try to rectify the mistake, but he claimed that I must have somehow, perhaps without realizing it, given some sign to the auctioneer that I wanted them. The only compromise offered was that the auctioneer would not want to be paid for a month the sum of around £15-£20. This practical joke at my expense was continued until the end of the month when Elvet Powell confessed that he and a few of his friends had set me up.

Nurse Davies was honoured with the B.E.M. by the Queen for her dedicated services to the people of the local parishes. She was revered by everyone as a devoted and highly efficient nurse. How she managed to get to distant farms, often in winter when snow was lying deep on the roads and lonely pathways leading to the upland isolated dwellings, is a mystery and a great tribute to her courage and professionalism. Among those most vociferous in her praise was Dai Jones who kept the shop at Abergwesyn. He had been a shepherd on the hills around Abergwesyn for over fifty years while his wife, who hailed from Dowlais, had kept the village shop and Post Office for the same period.

Thirty years later, I called with Professor Sir Glanmor Williams at the Abergwesyn Post Office, the home of eighty-year-old Dai Jones who had been a shepherd all his life, a keen eisteddfodwr and rope-maker from horse hair gathered on the local fences. We sat before a blazing fire surrounded by a Welsh dresser dripping with lustre jugs, pewter mugs and plates and a mahogany table covered with a crocheted cloth and a black Bible. In front of us was a mantelpiece with ten brass candlesticks on each side of a brown-framed mirror. Under the window was a long sofa draped in a red, plush velvet coverlet touching the coconut matting floor. Pale sun-bleached curtains dropped languidly from a thick brown rod, allowing a narrow view of the mountains, black and enormous, rounded and curved by low grey mists and cloud driven from the south.

Dai, like most mountain men, was lean, wire-sinewed, sharp-boned with a wind-weathered complexion and shrewd eyes lying deep and shadowed. He had spent his life tramping the waterlogged, fog-covered moorland which folded into little snow-choked valleys and swallow-holes in winter. This is where demons shrieked shrill descants on the white hills stabbing the frozen air, where ridged snow hid silent sheep. He had carried lambs down when the towering hills, silent and ominous, fell asleep, and he sought the shelter of the guttering flame in the lighted farm amid the sentinel trees. He had searched for lost sheep alone on jagged ledges, under mounds of drifted snow, digging and pulling and carrying them away from pinnacles of buttressed rock, surrounded by the skirmishing snowflakes and the razor-sharp wind. Then, when the seasons changed and Spring thawed the dumb stream, it became alive again, gurgling, tumbling under black, overhanging banks of peat and falling down its staircase course to the green valley below, making Dai a happier man. He had weathered years of March winds that carry the myriad plaintive cries of anxious, bleating ewes scenting and searching for lost lambs, fearful of the flapping carrion crows and ravens with their hard eyes and resonant bark. Overhead, searching buzzards rode lazily on thermals, watching and mewing down corridors of sunlight breaking through the scudding clouds, racing endlessly before keen winds and the hurrying mists on snow-capped summits. Then suddenly came Summer, warm and the air golden, the earth is soft and lush with cinquefoils, whinberries, pepperboxes and mushrooms in the little green oases amid the heather, and the tufted yellow pods of gorse. Now the black pools were dry and cracked, as curlews glided to the heath, and ringed ouzels hidden in the mountain ash trees, gave back life to the deserted hafotai, now green lichen dressed, fretted and eroded by rain and sun. Autumn brought the squalls of migrating birds on berried and leaf-undressing trees. He watched the moorland putting on the robe of dried yellow, which it had been its dress for millions of years, and the first fall of snow from leaden skies, red at sundown.

These mountains bruised by shadows, gales and sun had been his companions, they were his lost childhood, his work and refuge from the storms of life, his escape and fulfilment, his inspiration for poetry and music. It was here with the dawn chorus of birds and the morning sunlight reflected in dewdrops sparkling like jewels in the silence of human voices and the distant hills reaching up in prayer that he found God. It was here, nebulous in the moonlight, where the owl called a long shivering cry, where few men walked, that he looked down into the valley with its scattered farmsteads, where men and women struggled in endless toil to gain a living from a barren soil.

It was this environment of steep-sided mountains, moorland plateaux, rugged paths, loneliness and a harsh climate with hard winters spent on the hills for a pittance, which had shaped his character and personality. He was a happy man and this was reflected in his jovial temperament, his ever-ready smile and compassion for those suffering bereavement, illness or poverty. In spite of little education he was well- versed in the scriptures, poetry and music. He could recall who had won prizes in eisteddfodau years previously, naming the piece of music or poetry with which they had succeeded. His first language was Welsh, and what leisure time he had was devoted to choral singing at Llanwrtyd and preparing for musical competitions.

Professor Sir Glanmor Williams was with me in 1980, to check out my research for a doctorate. He sat intently listening to Dai's reminiscences of his childhood when he attended the local school, now closed and of his delight in poetry and music. Glanmor, who is an eminent Welsh historian, conversed with him on the merits of the Welsh poets, analyzing and criticizing as equals the older and contemporary poets such as Crwys. It was quite obvious that Glanmor was surprised to find a shepherd in such a remote area of Wales so cultured. After about an hour, when I was a passive listener to this entrancing conversation, Glanmor thanked him for his hospitality and told him that he regretted not having met him before. He said, "I was at the grave of Theophilus Evans at Llangamarch recently."

"Oh," said Dai, "I've read his Drych y Prif Oesoedd many times."

I then turned to Dai and in Welsh asked him if he ever went to Llanwrtyd, about six miles away.

"Yes," he replied, "I still cycle down to choir practice once a week."

"Do you ever go to Beulah?" I asked.

"Although it's only five miles down the valley," he said, "I haven't been there for years."

"Why is that?" I asked.

"Well", he said, lowering his voice almost to a whisper, "there were a gang of scoundrels living there thirty odd years ago."

"Were there" I said, rather surprised because at that time I was the schoolmaster there.

"Do you know," said Dai, as he pulled on his home-made pipe, "this gang used to come round all the villages about here on a Christmas time, when we had poultry whist drives and they would win all the prizes."

"And furthermore," he said, looking at Glanmor who was my senior examiner, "Bowen the schoolmaster was one of them!"

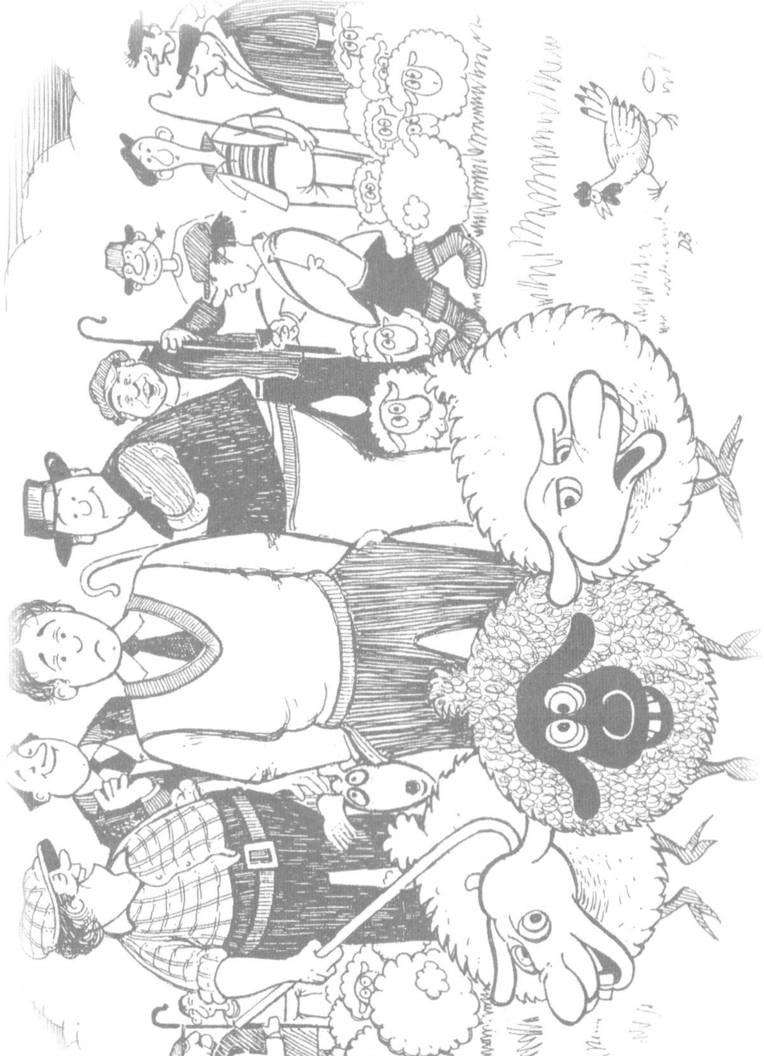

Kicking Out the Squire

ONE OF MY LASTING memories of my early days at Beulah school were the dinnertimes, when I had to do the necessary cooking, albeit primitive and rudimentary in the extreme. I was clearly aware of my very limited culinary skills as there was a lack of finesse and an unpalatable colour and taste to the food I cooked. Nevertheless, some discerning and experienced cooks among my fourteen-year-olds chuckled at my attempts to boil water, cook home-cured bacon and heat tins of beans. We cooked on the top of the tortoiseshell stove, which was then the only standard means of heating the schools. Although inartistic in appearance, they provided sufficient heat even on the coldest days, and required no servicing. They provided the only means of cooking and the radiant heat also dried the wet coats and stockings of children who walked from distant farms.

At mealtimes every child was provided with free hot cocoa, and they tucked into their sandwiches and even my cooking with enthusiasm, having not eaten for many hours and with appetites sharpened by the morning air and long journey to school. They joked and jested and buried their faces in chubby hands to hide their impish smiles, as they scrutinized me through their fingers. While lost in their eating, they irradiated that innocent and enchanting happiness of childhood freed from the terrors of the outer world. John Davies, the caretaker's grandson, generated paroxysms of laughter, even from the sad-faced little girl whose only previous companions had been the mountain sheep and dogs on her remote hill-farm.

After lunch the children poured forth into the uneven earthen yard, running in the sheer delight of innocent happy childhood friendships. They had to rely on their own resources; their play equipment was limited to a small ball or a skipping rope. 'Touch' was a favourite game except when the boys played football or cricket. The deep-rutted yard did not permit them to play marbles, hoop, tal-y-bimp, whips and tops or scotch which were played in the urban schools of South Wales. They played in the grass and on tree-stumps, sat under the beech trees in summer, and revelled in the companionship of school friends living in the village or on farms. The only change in this pastoral scene came in winter, when the fields, hedges and hills fell silently asleep under snow and the countryside shrouded, cold, forlorn and mysterious occasionally stopped the farm children from coming to school. On these days, the black trees and wild hedges stood out against the backcloth of quilted whiteness stretching to the leaden sky on the far-flung horizon. On these days children left school early, wrapped warm, capped and gloved. Then a mute, cathedral silence fell upon the classrooms, where other generations had laughed and learnt, before venturing into different worlds of sun-bathed shores, or to die in hostile lands across the seas.

Around 1949 I received a letter informing me that a school canteen was to be provided by the Education Authority. I was later informed that a porch at the school was to be modified, a new water-supply was to be provided and a school cook was to be appointed during the current term, to begin duties the following September. Within days a water diviner appeared, carrying a thin Y-shaped hazel-stick, about two feet long under his arm. He was in appearance a countryman, short, broad-shouldered and red faced under black, bushy eyebrows overhanging his smiling and intelligent eyes.

"Are you the Headteacher?" he asked with a soft Welsh lilt, so gentle in its intonation. His general demeanour suggested a man given to thinking, unobtrusive in approach and gentle in manner.

"I've come to search for water," he added.

"Where are you going to look for it?" I asked.

"I am instructed to test a field adjoining the school," he said.

"Oh, I know, follow me, please," I said and led him around the school, over the hedge and into a rather boggy field to the north of the school.

"There's plenty of water here," he said, "but we need to find the source. A well here would have a good downward flow to the school."

With that he held his fork-shaped hazel-stick firmly in front of him with both hands. Immediately the pointed end started to quiver and after some fifteen minutes of methodically covering the field, the stick bent downwards and it was obvious that he was experiencing some difficulty in holding the forked ends. He marked the spot with a wooden stake which he hammered into the soft ground.

"How do you do this?" I asked.

"I don't know," he said. "My father did this before me and his father before him," he said. "It seems to be some sort of gift."

"An important gift too," I replied, "when one realizes that somehow that ordinary-looking piece of hazel can tell you where there is a well of water."

"There's nothing special about the stick," he said, "except that hazel and fork-shaped."

"Could I try it?" I asked. "Yes, have a go," he said and handed me the stick.

"Hold it firmly and parallel to the ground like this," he added. He demonstrated how it should be used. I held it and walked a few steps but found that instead of pointing downwards it turned upwards and although holding it with all my strength, it bent over my right shoulder with such force that I was unable to hold it and when I released it, it fell some feet behind me. I was by now perspiring with my vain efforts to resist this strange force which had torn the stick out of my hands. He said nothing but, with a slight smile, picked the stick off the ground.

"I haven't your gift," I said. "No," he replied without giving any further comments or explanation. He walked from the damp field towards the school.

"Rushes will tell you where there's water," he said. I felt that there was more to finding water than just using the divining rod, and that was to know where to look by knowing the botanical plants and their habitat.

I realized that the school managers of my Non-Provided School would soon make an appointment of a school cook. I made it known to the Vicar and Minister that I favoured Mrs

Prosser and familiarized them with her crying need for help which would be assuaged by this appointment. I heard nothing further but waited for any news of an impending decision. I was not asked to attend any meeting because, in fairness to the managers, only they had the power to appoint.

In the village one tended to meet, in face-to-face situations, the same people every day, either in the shops, the Post Office or on the road. The number of cars was limited by petrol rationing, so I became aware of the fact that something was on when I spotted one evening the squire, the vicar, the minister and the estate agent passing through the village, over the bridge and up towards the school. I guessed immediately that they were proceeding to the school to make the appointment of the cook. I rushed up the hill and breathlessly arrived at the school gate, and there in the yard were their cars indicating that my assumption was correct.

I was infuriated to think that they were holding a meeting in the school without the prior consent of the authority. In taking this liberty they had revealed that there was another and far older authority operating here, and that was the all-powerful authority of the squire. Historically, of course, the squirearchy were the magistracy, the landowners with the power to evict, to terminate leases, and to imprison or to transport for life, on the most trivial excuses.

I made an unheralded entry and pretended surprise as I entered my classroom now filled with cigarette-smoke and jovial laughter. It was an untimely intrusion, and possibly a madcap decision lacking finesse and decorum to have barged in upon this meeting. The stentorian voice of one of the gathering suddenly stopped and there was a funereal silence when I said, "May I ask what is going on here, please?"

"We're holding a meeting," replied the squire resplendent in an Irish tweed fawn jacket and puffing on a thick cigar.

"Have you had permission to hold this meeting in the school?" I asked.

There were intermittent coughs, bowed heads and glazed eyes

popping with incredulity at my arrogance. The red face of the Commander became purple, his eyes reflected both surprise and intense anger as he retorted, "Good God, man, my grandmother built this bloody school." He spoke now with fury and indignation. He gazed at me with the eyes of a former commander of a flotilla of destroyers reprimanding a naval rating.

"I don't care if your grandfather helped her," I responded. "You have no right to be in the school without the permission of the Education Committee."

"I'm Chairman of the Breconshire County Council," he shouted as he stood and glared at me.

"In that case you should know better," I replied. "Now will you please leave the school?"

With low mutterings from his irritated fellows, the assemblage pushed back their chairs, stood up and shuffled behind the tall, broad-shouldered Commander, son of an Admiral and himself a noted rugby player.

As the cars sped from the schoolyard, I realized that my misguided enthusiasm had expressed itself in discourteous behaviour to older men. My recalcitrant behaviour did me no credit. I had contravened the accepted traditional code of the countryside, and this really was the consummation of my ignorance of accepted customs, built up over the centuries between landowner and tenant. The apparent immediate cause of my unrestrained anger was the fact that the squire had disregarded the regulations concerning the letting of schools, but the latent reasons I suppose were an objection to the fact that the Llwyn Madoc gentry could own a number of estates, dozens of farms, a mansion at Llwyn Madoc and collieries in South Wales where my father and thousands of others had slaved for a pittance. In addition, or rather as a result of this vast wealth, the squire was able to enjoy a style of life which included living at his London home in the Autumn, on the French Riviera in the early Spring and then returning for the fishing and shooting in the late Spring. The latter was battue shooting when hundreds of hand-fed pheasants were slaughtered by his friends, as local farmers sons and farm servants did the beating. I was told that this peasant labour was necessary if a son or servant aspired to have a farm on the estate after marriage.

My spontaneous reaction was also founded upon hearsay which likened them to the tyrannical Merthyr ironmasters, and to my reading which frequently described the gentry or squirearchy as absentee landlords and aliens in religion, politics and language from the Welsh peasantry. Carousel and pleasure were among their chief aims, they impoverished the land which they had usurped through fraud, craftiness and oppression. Upon reflection, however, only some of these accusations were probably true, but I should have brought an unprejudiced mind to bear on this subject, and my reading of the Minutes of Evidence of the Land Commission which sat from 1893 to 1895, and of the Blue Books or the South Wales Squires by Herbert M. Vaughan, might have produced a more balanced appraisal of their worth. Vaughan, who was of a gentry dynasty himself, paid the most flowing tributes to Miss Clara Thomas, aunt of the present squire of Llwyn Madoc, when he stated, "She offered perhaps the highest example in every good sense of the Welsh squires ... she was stately and handsome. Kindness and sympathy beamed from her face ... she taught in the Sunday School at Llwyn Madoc ... never a day passed without some act of kindness or help to poorer neighbours ... she was the simplest and easiest of mortals ... her wealth was shared with those less liberally endowed and she could speak some Welsh. She also built the school and Eglwys Oen Duw Church at Beulah." These remarks were confirmed by the older generation who had known Miss Thomas and likewise references made about the squires of Llwyn Madoc were always most complimentary. Miss Clara Thomas died on 12 June 1914 and Vaughan wrote thus of his old friend; "A long reign of beneficence and practical piety has come to an end: the tyranny of the Welsh squires that had enthralled the valley of the Camarch for over 40 years was at last finished and done with."

A verse of the eulogy written by the Reverend Gethin Griffith, Vicar of Llandefalle, praised her life thus:

"God gave her wealth, and with it, gift more rare,
A loving sympathy and heart to care,
For poor and needy, and with them to share
   The very best."

It is ironic that the cook of my choice was eventually appointed, and after a brief introductory period proved to be excellent. I was very glad of this because in my naivity, I had considered her circumstances far more important than her cooking expertise. In the midst of this euphoria for her ability we had a rather unpleasant experience. I had been aware almost from the very beginning of her cooking career at the school, that every meal involving some liquid, whether gravy or stew, always had small white cylindrical objects about a centimetre long floating about on the surface. One day without thinking of anything in particular, I lifted one out on to the edge of my plate. In looking at it I was astonished to find that it was a white maggot. When I drew the attention of the cook to these things, she informed me that they were coming through the tap water! I ran to the well, lifted the uneven iron lid and found three maggot-infested, decomposing rabbits floating on the black well water. The well was cleaned out and a new lid was provided and the school dinners continued to be enjoyed by staff and pupils alike.

On the topic of white objects, Vaughan refers to the llaethfaen or milk-stone which was kept at Llwyn Madoc. As he states, "This was a chalky stone or lump that was supposed to possess certain powers of healing which was obtained by scraping some powder off the stone and then drinking it in milk. The people around Llwyn Madoc (1926) were, as I have already said, primitive folk and even in the early years of the twentieth century some of them were said to have recourse to this llaethfaen from time to time. But there was a strict taboo on the whole subject of the llaethfaen and its uses." Vaughan was correct because I heard no mention of it during my time at Beulah.

One may ask why old folk-customs such as that associated with the llaethfaen have disappeared. One explanation is that the Welsh countryside has become less and less peasant-like in those characteristics which enabled old customs to linger on. No longer are the countryside communities the intimate little worlds they were in the last century. Nevertheless, I heard vague references to Beulah people having seen ghostly funeral processions and y cannwyll corff (corpse candle), prior to a death.

I noted considerable activity among the young men in October, and much of the conversation was of salmon-catching or spotting females laying eggs in the rivers and the making or acquiring of gaffs. This was a six-foot rod with a large metal barb on the end. The method of poaching salmon was to spot them during the day laying their eggs and bedding down among the shingle or stones in the river. Then, at night, two men or boys would search, one carrying a torch to shine onto the salmon and the other the gaff. This would then be passed over the body of the salmon and then pulled powerfully into its side. If this operation was successful the fish was pulled out of the water onto the bank and killed.

It was at this time that I received an invitation to supper with Mr and Mrs Elvet Powell of Maesllech. After supper we sat around the hearth which for centuries has been the traditional scene of recreation and entertainment in rural Wales. Eventually, we came around to the supernatural and specifically to the phenomenon called y cannwyll corff, whereby a ghostly candle would move from a farmhouse or along a road or lane prior to a death. Elvet cited a case in his own family where old Jim, his servant man, at present eating in the back kitchen, had seen y cannwyll corff (the corpse candle) on the Maesllech lane late at night some years previously. This light had followed a peculiar pattern in that it had come towards him, struck an oak post, veered across the lane and then through the hedge into a field on his right.

When he reported this incident to Elvet's family he was informed that Elvet's sister had been taken ill. She died the following day and when the cortège was proceeding down the lane a few days later, one of the bearers slipped, the coffin draped in black struck the oak gate-post and passed through the hedge into the field, as old Jim had seen the corpse candle do on the previous night. I left Maesllech between eleven and twelve o'clock and as I approached the oak gate I heard what I thought were children's cries. Suddenly a lane of daytime enchantment with its steep banks topped by trees became overburdened with this frenzy of hideous pitiful cries, resounding through the cold eerie blackness. I stood motionless, petrified by fear of the supernatural and expecting at any moment to be an unwilling witness to the corpse candle.

I identified the cries coming from what appeared to be a gnomic dance of whitish creatures crying, turning, rolling and twisting in the nearby field. When I had overcome my terror and entered the field, I discovered to my horror that the tumbling gnomes were rabbits struggling and heaving to free themselves from the grid iron, the steel jaws of gin-traps embedded in their legs. Wide-eyed in terror with flesh ravelled down to their paws, with white bones holding them to the traps, they writhed in agony. The green meadows had become hostile places of death and torture, inflicting pain on these poor creatures.

I moved quickly from one to the other, releasing these mangled creatures from their traps. Some tried vainly to hop on broken limbs, while others dragged themselves to their hedgerow burrows. I walked home sickened by this inordinate cruelty, acutely aware, too, of the agonized cries of other mutilated creatures in the nearby woods and fields. This barbarism was not a completely new insight into rural life. This really was nature 'red in tooth and claw'. The following morning one of my pupils asked me if I would like to purchase two chickens at ten shillings each. I readily agreed and she promised to bring them on Friday so that I could take them home to my family in Cefn Coed.

Thursday night was now my usual night for collecting my three pounds of Black Market butter and three dozen eggs. It was a dry October night, cold but tolerable, the sky dark with the moon revealing itself sporadically, lighting up the muddy pathway through the meadows of the vicarage. I hammered the massive front door and heard a shuffling of feet, a key being turned and the slow creak of the door. It opened into the long, dark passage leading into the many damp, sad rooms on the ground floor. Mrs Hawkins escorted me into the living room; I mentioned my experience with the gin-trapped animals, collected my contraband and left, taking the lane running parallel with the Annell brook.

I skirted the Aberannell farmhouse but disturbed the sheep dogs and hurried along the narrow lane in order to attend the concert being held at the village hall for the Homecoming Fund for local servicemen. Again the air was rent by the horrendous cries of trapped animals. I was wondering how long it would take for a trapped animal to die when I was suddenly made aware of a luminous moving light under the trees bordering the banks of the Annell brook on my right. "My God," I thought, this is a cannwyll corff (the corpse candle) that Elvet Powell had referred to. I stopped and moved to the side of the lane to perceive the moving light, now quite close to me. I accidentally caused a wire to vibrate in the fence, and immediately the light from the corpse candle shone into my face, totally blinding me in its glare.

"It's alright boys," said a youthful voice, "it's only Bowen schoolin."

I discerned three shadowy figures in the field between the fence and the brook and could faintly see three objects, writhing and jumping on the wet grass.

"What are those?" I enquired.

"Don't you know what salmon look like?" said a voice.

"No," I replied. "I've never seen live salmon before."

"Would you like one?" one of them enquired.

"Yes, please." He then asked, "Which one?"

"The middle one," I replied.

"Right then, go down to Miss Parry's and borrow her pinafore and bring your mackintosh as well," said the tallest of the three.

"I'll be back in twenty minutes," I replied and returned in a short time with the required garments.

"Wrap the salmon up in the pinafore lengthways," said the leader who obviously knew this routine.

"Now kneel down, put your hands through the pockets and catch the ends of the pinafore, stand up and we'll button you up."

I carried out their instructions and was able to walk away with this twelve-pound salmon tucked safely under my mackintosh. It slightly altered my gait as it swung against my thighs. Everything went according to plan until I came to the village hall where the first members of the audience were arriving for the concert, and where Police Sergeant Rees was making himself important by directing the few cars that had rationed petrol.

"Good-evening, Mr Bowen," he said. The conversation continued for some time in a convivial tone. Meanwhile the weight of the salmon was beginning to tell and my hands were aching with an intense pain that must have registered in my face or voice.

"I want to be seen," he said, "so that the poachers will think themselves safe tonight, but little do they know that all the keepers are out looking for them."

Frightened and in agony by now, I excused myself and disappeared into Miss Parry's house. I dropped the salmon onto the red-tiled floor. I discovered that it was a two- and-a-half-foot male fish, its perfect symmetry, silver scales and powerful fins destroyed by a gaping, rugged wound in its side. In accepting this forbidden, out-of season salmon, I had become a poacher. In the last century men had been transported for fourteen years for killing a rabbit on the squire's land. But then one has to know something about the normative values of the Welsh countryside before making critical comments about the peasantry or the landowners.

SWEET BEULAH LAND

The Gamekeeper and a Woodland Encounter

MUCH REMAINED IN THE village society of the nineteenth-century peasant culture of the gwerin or country folk. The keeping of a cow, fattening a pig, keeping poultry, and having a few rows of potatoes in a local farmer's field in return for harvest labour, still persisted.

My landlady, Miss Parry, enjoyed all the hard work associated with these peasant culture activities. With age, however, certain jobs proved to be too arduous and she found it necessary to seek help. She paid a nominal rent to the squire of two shillings and sixpence a week for a substantial three-bedroomed brick house, a cowshed, barn, pigsty, large kitchen-garden and three acres of land. The large garden became a problem and to overcome the difficulty of sowing and harvesting, she employed John Davies, a seventy-year-old retired gamekeeper, to dig, sow and harvest her kitchen-garden.

John Davies was a short, dark-haired, clean-shaven man with a ruddy complexion typically dressed in cord trousers, an old black jacket and waistcoat with a collarless, flannel shirt worn Summer and Winter. Nature had endowed him with a serious, polite, refined manner and gentle mode of speech. He seemed to be condemned to a meek and lowly spirit that reflected a contemplative mind, one of those silent diffident souls. He was evidently a profound lover of nature, revelling in all its mysteries, with the hills and woods speaking to him of magic and beauty. It was so ironic that destiny had decided that to earn his daily bread his work required that he should breed and nurture pheasants, and to kill what was broadly called vermin, hawks, crows, magpies, stoats, weasels, foxes and polecats so that a few aristocrats should enjoy bloodsports. Undoubtedly retirement released him from this iniquity.

I was always delighted to see him digging the garden in

Springtime because it meant that after supper we could savour long discussions about wild life and old country customs and traditions. We spoke about his childhood in Beulah, about his family, about his work as a gamekeeper which involved the breeding and feeding of the young birds prior to their release for the shooting season. This was in the Spring when the squire would invite a number of friends down to Llwyn Madoc, and when young men from the estate farms would act as beaters. When I referred to this aspect of his work his demeanour and the slow shaking of his head suggested a degree of sadness which implied that his life's work had been really a waste of time and energy. There was, too, the thought that he had been engaged in the business of indirectly killing God's creatures to satisfy man's blood-lust. A good day would be when a hundred brace of birds were shot by the squire's friends.

In talking about old customs, he referred to folk medicines and cited his recent facial skin rash, which the local doctors had failed to cure. Remembering what he had heard as a child on his grandmother's hearth about the medicinal qualities of ground ivy for skin complaints, he decided to try it.

"What did you do to prepare this medicine?" I asked.

"Very simply," he replied, "I gathered a bag full of ground ivy in the woods, washed it thoroughly and then boiled it for a few hours."

"And then I suppose you made some kind of poultice, did you?" I asked.

"No!" he replied "I drained off the fluid and when it had cooled, I bathed my face with it by dabbing it with a clean handkerchief."

"How bad was your face?" I asked.

"It was very inflamed and covered with sores matted into my beard because I couldn't shave," he replied.

"How good then was the ground ivy?" I asked.

"I found it soothing my face immediately," he replied, "and furthermore in a few days the sores dried up and fell off."

"Well, something similar happened to the Reverend

Theophilus Evans, vicar of Llangamarch, who, on a Sunday morning in 1732, while walking to Llanwrtyd, drank from the stinking well and cured himself of scurvy which had been troubling him for months," I said.

"Exactly the same kind of complaint," he added, "and of course, he in a way established the now well-known Spas at Llanwrtyd."

"Theophilus Evans of course was the author of Drych y Prif Oesoedd, which went to thirty editions in the eighteenth century. His grandson was the famous Theophilus Jones, who wrote the History of Brecknock in 1805," I added.

"I think you are right," he replied, as he pulled on his pipe in reflective mood. "Do you know, Bowen bach, the old people were so poor, they couldn't afford to have a doctor. Look at the plant names around here - Herb Robert and Self Heal," he said.

"Well, that's very interesting," I said. "Tell me, Mr Davies, with all the time you've spent in the woods and on the hills, have you ever experienced any strange happenings?"

"Well, it all depends what you mean by 'strange'," he said. "For example, I saw a rabbit running into the fold at Esgaircoedifor, stopping and crying like a baby. Then a few moments later a stoat came around the corner which had probably been following it for days, jumped on its back, buried its teeth in the nape of the rabbit's neck, drank its blood and killed it. Do you know, the rabbit didn't try to escape."

"It didn't make any effort to run away?" I asked.

"No, it just stayed there and was killed. But talking of stoats, I was walking up the lane from the church one morning when I rounded a bend and found the lane full of stoats coming towards me."

"What did you do?"

"I ran for my life because they would have killed me." They say that packs of stoats move from one farm to another. When they've killed all the rabbits in one place they'll move on to the next."

I found this particularly interesting because at home in Cefn

Coed, Mr Morgan John of the Ffrwd had told me that his father had seen a long column of rats crossing a lane in the Penmoelallt Woods. Similarly, in the company of my brother and Mr David Sivil, the farmer at Coed Owen, Cwm Taf, I saw dozens of large grey rats eating from the pigs' troughs there one Autumn afternoon. There were so many that when he fired both barrels of his double-barrelled gun at them, he killed twenty-seven. They dispersed but within ten minutes there were just as many there again. However, when I asked him some weeks later about the number of rats on his farm, he informed me that they had disappeared overnight. The record, so I am informed, for the highest number of rats killed in one day is held by Mr Arthur Sayce of Trefechan, Cefn Coed, who killed over four hundred at the Cwm Pontsticill in the 1980s. From the evidence, it would appear that stoats and rats migrate in large numbers, probably in search of food.

I had seen dozens of grass snakes and adders in my youth and was interested to know whether there were many in this locality. John Davies stated that he had seen some during his lifetime but not many. I then told him that two men, Mr Morgan John of the Ffrwd, Cefn Coed and a grave-digger at Cefn Coed Cemetery, had witnessed large numbers of snakes together waving their heads as if in a dance. Mr John had seen dozens together in a swallow-hole on Penmoelallt mountain around a large flat stone upon which lay a snake between five and six feet long. The grave-digger had seen them under the conifer trees near the cemetery only on one occasion. In view of the large numbers of snakes in this vicinity at Cefn Coed, it is a wonder that others had not seen and recorded this strange phenomenon. The response to these strange happenings by Mr John Davies of Beulah, who ran for his life, and that of the grave-digger, were rather different. When I asked the grave-digger how he had responded to the dozens of dancing snakes he replied, "Oh I did nothing because there was a five-strand fence between us so it was alright!"

"What would you have done, Mr Davies," I asked, "if you'd seen this strange spectacle of so many snakes involved in this sort of dance?"

"Well, to tell you the truth, I've not seen many snakes, and thank goodness for that," he said, "because I'm terrified of them. I would probably have fired my shotgun into the middle of them and ran for my life."

After finishing his supper John left and I realized that most households and certainly every farmer had a shotgun of sorts in Beulah. This was to exterminate pests such as foxes or carrion crows, which attacked young lambs in Springtime. In addition, guns provided food in the form of rabbits and hares or pigeons. Rabbits were also shot as a means of income, and were sold to hucksters who collected them from the farms. Rabbits were so numerous and did so much damage that shooting them thus served two purposes. Shooting appeared to me to be a far more humane method of disposing of them than by using the barbaric gin-traps which were so commonly used.

I had spent the whole of August in Cefn Coed and returned to Beulah in early September, and on the Thursday of the first week back in school I went to the vicarage to collect my weekly ration of butter and eggs. As I entered the hall, the air filled with the most appealingly delicious aroma of some tasty dish.

"That's an appetising smell Mrs Hawkins," I commented as I walked into the lounge where the table was already set for a meal.

"We've got rabbit stew," she said. "Come and join Brynley and myself." With that, Brynley, who had just come into the room, said, "Yes, come on, sit down. I shot two rabbits this morning and there's plenty for all of us in the pot." I sat down and was soon enjoying a delectable meal.

"This is absolutely beautiful soup," I said. "I wouldn't mind taking a few rabbits home with me this weekend."

"Well, if you've had enough why don't you borrow my gun and go out now and get a couple before dark? There's plenty up on Cefn Cardis, they've eaten well in my garden this year," he said as he walked to his sideboard and handed me his gun and five cartridges.

Within fifteen minutes I had walked from the vicarage through Aberannell and was soon on Cefn Cardis Road, so called because for centuries this was the road used by the Cardiganshire Drovers (Cardis) en route with their cattle through mid-Wales for the English fairs and markets. It was now grass-covered and led along the ridgeway from Abergwesyn to Beulah and thence to Llanafan Fawr and Newbridge-on-Wye, before crossing to the English border. At Beulah and along the route there were blacksmiths' shops where the cattle could have replacement shoes if required. Prior to starting, the cattle had two shoes nailed on each foot, pigs had leather shoes, while geese had their feet dipped in hot tar and were then made to walk on sand to protect their feet on the long journey to England.

My first rabbit was a sitting target and shooting it demanded no skill whatsoever. When I bent down to pick it up, however, I saw that its head was a mass of moving fleas and its ears were filled with the insects, and this probably accounted for the rabbit not hearing my approach. I had heard of this phenomenon and that when the body became cold the fleas would vanish. I left the rabbit and moved quietly along Cefn Cardis Road, admiring the majestic mountain scenery and the lake, where in the Spring thousands of wild daffodils had enchanted me and reminded me of Wordsworth's poem.

Suddenly, the silence was disturbed by the unmistakable raucous screech of a cock-pheasant in the field immediately on my right. I peered through the pleached green hedge, and there he was strutting proudly with his harem of eight or so hens following behind his lordship.

As I ruminated on whether I should take a shot at this beautiful bird, I was aware historically of the poaching wars between landowners and peasantry that had persisted for centuries. It was a guerrilla war, spasmodically waged, both sides believing that it had God and Right on its side, each nourishing an intense hatred of the other. Each side had its own code of conduct and honour, its own specific weaponry of 'swingels', iron poacher stoppers, spears, camouflaged pits, booby-traps, man-traps and swivelling spring-guns. Most of the magistrates were landowners and one way of ensuring that poachers were removed from the immediate locality was to transport them to America, Tasmania or Australia. People such as Hugh Price of Brecon, for example, had been transported for fourteen years for sheep-stealing; Job Pritchard of Llanfihangel Nant-brân was transported for fourteen years for stealing a mare, while Brilliana Thomas of Brecon was transported for seven years for stealing a spoon.

I killed the cock-pheasant with my second shot, crossed the gate and very slowly walked across the field. I casually picked up the bird and then dropped it in a clump of brown ferns, intending to collect it later on my return, and when it was darker and safer. It was nearly dark when I returned but the pheasant had gone. Was someone playing a trick on me or had it been picked up by someone who had been watching me or had heard my two shots? While both annoyed and mystified by the disappearance of the pheasant, I had learnt yet another lesson in country life. But then there might have been quite an innocent explanation: maybe a predator from the woods below me on his twilight search for food had scented it. These conjectures were abruptly ended when I heard piercing screams ripping through the darkening wood. I forgot about my pheasant and, with my gun in one hand, I climbed over the fence and slithered down the green embankment towards the pitiful screams. I followed a winding track under the canopy of trees and into a small clearing where a girl, poorly dressed and mentally slow, stood pointing hysterically at her howling dog, dragging on the short chain of a gin trap, closed on one if its torn paws.

It was a huge young dog, and its upturned snout clearly indicated that its father was the vicar's bull mastiff. The dog was massive and I was aware that it was fiercely protective of this poor girl. I lowered my gun, tried vainly to calm the girl and spoke gently to the dog now baring its teeth and growling both in pain and anger as I crawled towards him. He tore at the chain as he pulled away on his haunches, slipping and snapping as I came nearer and nearer to his fearsome dribbling jaws. Wild-eyed and snarling on his two-foot chain, he cried in pain, and then with my shoulder towards him I gradually opened the grid iron jaws buried in his bleeding leg. Suddenly, he was free and on three legs he limped to his mistress and licked her hand and, to my amazement, crawled deferentially towards me and similarly licked mine. I walked with them to the village, leaving behind my flea-ridden rabbit and that beautiful cock-pheasant, fully aware now that the common belief among townspeople that nothing happens in the countryside is totally untrue. In one evening I had had three strange experiences and the dog which previously snarled at anyone venturing too near his handicapped mistress always greeted me henceforth by running towards me and licking my hand. This I found very strange because of his well-known malevolent disposition towards strangers.

Primitive but Necessary

OUTSIDE THE WHITE-WASHED farmhouse door an old blind sheepdog lay in the shadows away from the May sun which shed its light over the remote farm and buildings. Apple-trees in the nearby garden bulged with bouquets of pink and white pendulous flowers which showered the perimeter walls and yard with whirling petals. Lying on this carpet of snow, swollen and bloated, grunted a mud-spattered sow, snorting oblivious to the litter of pink squat piglets running around her bulging belly.

"Come on, Siân, move yourself," said a tall farm worker, strong and ruddy- faced, deeply lined by unremitting toil on this upland farm.

"Hello, Mr Bowen, is it?" he asked.

"I've come up for the pig," I replied.

"Here he is," he said. "Come and have a look at him, he's a real beauty Jim Evans picked him for you, six pounds if you're taking him."

"Oh yes, I'm taking him, I've got a friend with a car up there," I said, pointing towards the road. "Here's the money."

"I'll put him in a sack for you," he said as he bent down in the sty and caught the squealing mass of kicking legs and dropped him into the sack.

I tried to appear used to this kind of operation and swung the sack and pig over my shoulder and carried this squirming, kicking bundle of livestock up to the car.

"Have you tied the sack?" asked Ralph, who was waiting by the car. He could see that in spite of my apparent acquired rural skills, I was still an amateur in these matters.

"Here," he said, "tie him up or he'll be running around in the boot."

I tied the neck of the sack, lowered him into the boot and within minutes we were on the return journey from this isolated dwelling in the Abergwesyn Valley. The road rose and fell, turned and twisted under the canopy of a cloudless sky as we wove through the majestic bare-topped hills with wooded slopes and irregular fields dotted with sheep and lambs and grazing cattle. We descended to the silent Dolfelin Mill, triangular in plan, sad, slated and sombre with worn-out millstones leaning against the random stone walls. The car chugged up the wooded slope from Dolfelin Mill which revealed Llwyn Madoc mansion, which was a white mock- Elizabethan house with black wooded bay windows symmetrically distributed across the front elevation. Behind a vertical tree-covered rock-face towered over the house providing in the Spring an awesomely beautiful canopy of foliage with perfect lawns running down to the Camarch brook. This was a manor-house dating probably from the nineteenth century, aping its English counterpart even to the gardens contiguous to it. Charlie Smith was one of the gardeners here; his wages were less than two pounds a week in 1945 with a cottage behind the shop for half-a-crown a week.

While these spacious fertile gardens provided vegetables for Llwyn Madoc house, the butter, cheese, bacon and lamb came from the home farm tenanted by Mr Lamacraft, who was the estate agent or manager. Traditionally estates in Wales had English managers who were responsible for rents, repairs, tenancies and so on. They also acted as a buffer between the squire and his tenants and in reality were part of the anglicization process which over centuries tended to separate the aristocracy from the peasantry. Many of these landlords were strangers in their own land and their ignorance of Welsh life made it difficult for them to play an active part in it. They could be little more than patrons of a culture which existed apart from them with the religious revivals of the eighteenth and nineteenth centuries and the development of Nonconformity among the gwerin (peasantry), the separation between the world of landlord and tenant became virtually complete. The religious awakening stimulated political and national consciousness and the landlord became increasingly identified with the ancien régime. As a class, the aristocracy supported the Church and resented the

Nonconformity of their tenants. When I arrived at Beulah in 1945, however, there was no evidence of any conflict between the squire and the local people. I noticed that the men doffed their hats, or touched their caps, when the squire passed in his car, and any references made to the squire were always couched in terms of respect. The old dichotomy, if it had existed here, was not overt.

We paused at the road junction with one road leading to the former Dolaeron woollen mill and the other to Beulah. On our left between these roads was Eglwys Oen Duw, a Church of dignified proportions built in the last century by the present squire's aunt, Miss Sarah Thomas. She was a much-respected lady among the older generation for her good works among her tenants in the neighbouring hamlets and parishes. The spired church and stained-glass windows were in harmony with the mellow radiance and quietude of its charming interior and the peaceful churchyard outside.

We arrived at the Beulah Post Office and I carried my kicking piglet into the sty at the rear. I lowered him down gently, opened the sack and the black and white saddle back squealed and kicked his way into his new domain. Jim's pig, which was larger, sniffed, nudged and pushed this intruder which protested and escaped into the darkness and safety of the rear covered end. He soon settled and when I brought him a mixture of river water, meal and potatoes an hour later he competed hungrily and successfully with his older colleague for every mouthful of swill.

Jim Evans, the Post Mistress's husband, worked in a Builth garage and we arranged for him to feed the pigs every morning except on weekends while I would do likewise in the nights. Everything worked marvellously well until October when both pigs were now quite large and almost ready to kill.

It was at the end of October that the Kitson Motor Cycle trials were held at Builth. I decided to compete and the day before I told Jim Evans that I would be coming up from Merthyr for the trials because by now I was a real motorcycle enthusiast. I enjoyed the power and speed of a motorcycle which my cars have lacked. Saturday came and as I passed the Lion Garage in Builth, Jim was waiting for me with dreadful news, that I might soon be without a pig.

"Hey," he said, "you'd better get up to Beulah as fast as you can. We had a cloudburst up in Abergwesyn and the river has overflowed its banks at Beulah and your pig is trapped in its sty."

I didn't wait to ask about his pig. I immediately cancelled my visit to the motorcycle trials, drove out of Builth and headed for Beulah, some fourteen miles away. By the time I arrived in the village the waters had receded and I was able to get to the sty without any difficulty. There in the forecourt of the sty lay my pig with outstretched legs, glazed eyes, panting irregularly but still alive. I wondered what on earth I could do. He was far too large for me to move him into the covered area of the sty. I boiled some milk and tried to restore him with warm spoonfuls which merely dribbled out of his mouth. I covered him with dry sacks and then wondered whether one of the village shops sold a pig medicine. I went across to Mrs Davies who was the nearer of the two shopkeepers.

"Hello, Mrs Davies, I wonder if you can help me," I said. "My pig has been trapped under water since yesterday in his sty and is barely alive. Have you anything that might revive him?"

"Well, the only thing that I have is a general animal medicine, whether this will revive him or not I don't know," she replied.

"Oh, I'll take that. How much is it please?"

"Four shillings and eleven pence halfpenny."

By now it was almost dark and with the greatest difficulty I read 'One dessert spoonful ....'? I couldn't read the rest of the instructions, so after getting the appropriate spoon from my landlady, I inserted a large dessert spoon full of the deep blood-red mixture into his mouth. I was totally unprepared for his reaction. He shot two feet into the air and raced like a comet around the sty so fast that at times it appeared he was racing like a motorcyclist around the wall of death. No greyhound or deer had ever travelled at this speed. It was quite astonishing and continued for some minutes until, at last, he slithered to a halt with legs outstretched, gasping and foaming what appeared to be blood from his gaping mouth. This continued until his snout was submerged with his forelegs under a pillow of red foam.

I concluded that he was now in his death-throes and would soon die, so I decided to return the medicine to the shopkeeper if she would take it back. I explained to her what had happened and probably feeling sorry for me said, "Oh, don't worry Mr Bowen, here's your money."

"I only gave him a spoonful and I think it's killed him," I said.

As I was speaking to her I was looking at the instructions, and in the bright light of the Aladdin lamp hanging from the ceiling of her shop I could now read the first line of the instructions which stated: 'One dessert spoonful in a gallon of water' ! I blush even now with shame when I recall that I had given that poor pig one dessert-spoonful neat. I left the shop confused by it all and went over the road to take what I thought would be my last look at my pig before burying it on Monday, when I returned from Cefn Coed after my weekend at home.

On Monday I arrived at Beulah, just as the first signs of morning light were appearing over the sleeping village shrouded in river mist and silence. Frost provided a strange whiteness to the earth and grass, frost-spiked trees hung their branches heavy and gaunt, as my feet crushed the crisp earthen pathway to the sty. I peered over the low stone wall and the pig, now covered in a thick layer of hoar-frost, grunted an acknowledgement of my arrival. He was alive so I decided that I should phone for the vet. I informed him of the symptoms and we arranged to meet at eleven o'clock at the sty.

He arrived promptly, a pleasant, round-faced, dark-eyed, square-shouldered man who was obviously busy and eager to see my pig. Using a stethoscope and thermometer he was quick in his diagnosis.

"Your pig has swine erysipelas as a result of being in the flood water," he said. "It has a very high temperature. Give him these tablets and arrange for him to be killed immediately. You will receive my bill – shall I address it to the school?" he asked. I replied in the affirmative and within minutes he had gone and I was left with the problem of finding someone to kill the pig as soon as possible. I returned to school with a severe headache and acute depression. That evening I called upon Mr Edgar Davies, my neighbour at Glan-yr-Afon, and explained my difficulties to him.

"Kill it immediately ... that's a load of rubbish to start with. Look," he said, "go to the shop and buy a pound of Epsom salts, a pound of Glauber Salts and a pint of olive oil. Put them all in Miss Parry's saucepan and boil them up."

"What do I do after?" I asked.

"Find an old wellington and cut a hole in the toe and bring a length of rope with you and I'll meet you in the sty about six o'clock. I'll bring a lantern," he said.

"What if I can't find a wellington?" I asked.

"Find an old working boot instead," he said. He was clearly annoyed with the vet's diagnosis and was now bringing forth the secret lore of the countryside, where peasantry were forced by poverty to experiment and innovate in a largely self-sufficient community. Edgar was a tall, heavily built man, fleshy and red-faced and as strong as an ox.

"Don't be late, six o'clock sharp. Do you understand?" he added brusquely.

I felt myself coming alive again under the impetus of his instructions and scurried around the village collecting the items which he had designated as necessary for the rescue operation. By six o'clock I stood replete with all the items stacked against the sty wall. Inside, the pig, motionless but clearly visible in the moonlight, slumbered on oblivious of my anxiety and to the cold shroud of mist rising from the river, enveloping and silently obliterating the buildings and the canopy of trees. The austere bleakness and clammy cold air cast gloom and mystery over the scene where the silence was broken only by the river, a few yards away, gurgling with subdued anger under the alders and willows.

The click of the garden gate indicated the approach of my friend who emerged through the mist with his lantern, creating a halo of translucent light in the whirling mist.

"Got everything?" he asked as he quickly opened the sty door and moved towards the prone pig. He took my rope and made a noose which he slipped over its lower jaw.

"Here," he said, "tie this to the gatepost in case he starts struggling."

I tied the rope to the post thinking to myself that it would need a miracle to get the dying pig to struggle. My thoughts were interrupted by another command.

"When I open his mouth shove the toe of the wellington into his mouth, and pour the saucepan full of that stuff into the leg of the wellington."

"Right."

"I'll hold the wellington in his mouth, now pour it in."

I did this and to my amazement the pig started gulping down the warm liquid as he bit on the soft toe of the wellington.

"It's all gone," I said.

"Right, undo the rope and lift the door off the hinges. We'll roll him onto the door and carry him up to my barn and cover him with hay."

His barn was at the northern end of the village. We lifted him onto the door and then slowly, using knees and brute strength, we rose from the slimy floor with the makeshift bier, lantern and prostrate pig. The effort awakened all the robust reservoir of Edgar's energetic, full-blooded body as we walked slowly through the gloom of the night towards his barn. Perspiring, blowing and exhaling puffs of warm air into the mist, we finally arrived at the barn door, ajar and revealing a full barn, fragrantly filling the night air with the scent of new-mown hay. We shuffled forward, lowered our burden and then concealed it under a pyramid of hay.

"He'll be alright by the morning," claimed my friend confidently, with all the assurance of a man who had experienced this before and had succeeded in his cure. In my urban innocence I asked, "Will he suffocate under that load of hay?"

"No," he replied, "he'll be fine, you wait and see."

We closed the barn door. It was old, broken here and there, green with a sheen of lichen and held in position by rusted hinges and a latch probably made by the local blacksmith, Jim Mathias.

We walked away from the old building which had stored hay, been the secret trysting place for lovers and a lodging house for vagrants for centuries. Soon we crossed the bridge over the swirling Camarch and, turning to our respective homes, retired into the cosy warmth of the coal-fired kitchen with flames licking around the suspended kettles hanging on their hooks and chains. Under a perceptive barrage of probing questions, I slowly recounted the events of the night and was then glad to scent the delectable smell of Miss Parry's ham sizzling on the fire. She was an expert at curing her hams and, like Edgar Davies, had a lifetime's training and experience in acquiring the lore and old secrets of country people. Perhaps because of the frugality of their lives, the limitations imposed by home production of vegetables and meat necessitated a compensatory care and devotion to getting the best out of each morsel cooked. A meal of ham and eggs with home-made butter provided one of the most common and tasty meals for rural folk.

At half-past seven the following morning it was just beginning to get light when I marched steadfastly past the village hall, the Carpenters' Arms and cottages where lights were flickering in a few windows. Artisans on their way to the Estate workshops called "Good-morning!" as they rode silently along on their bicycles. The faint outline of the barn under the huge bare trees concealed in the dark haze of river fog, filled me with some anxiety and fear that my pig, in whom I had invested so much of my extremely limited financial resources, was dead. I tremulously lifted the latch, dragged the door open and heard a grunt which prompted me to pull harder and there standing, bright-eyed and clearly very hungry, was my pig.

I was delighted with his survival and marvelled at the manifest excellence of Edgar Davies's knowledge of animal folk medicines. I was gradually being made aware of an old tradition of folk medicines and of people who had the knowledge and skills and secrets handed down to them from one generation to another. I was aware of a science based on an amalgam of experience, experiment, success and failure, intuition, custom and tradition, extending over centuries of life in rural communities before veterinary science, as we know it today, was ever thought of. My eyes had been opened to this primitive art, and of facets of rural life steeped in the past of which I had no knowledge.

It was part of a rural tradition, too, that cottagers were permitted to gather wool from fences and bushes; it was an old custom called gwlana. Another custom was that those cottagers who helped with the harvest were allowed to grow a few rows of potatoes in with the farmer's crop, in return for services rendered. Jim Evans had this privilege and also that of gleaning the small potatoes left by the farmer to feed our pigs. Rural life depended upon the co-operation of farmers, craftsmen and the peasantry or cottagers. The granting of these privileges by farmers was indirectly a way of ensuring that the peasantry survived, many of whom were often barely surviving due to poverty, harsh weather and a poor soil. There can hardly be a more back-breaking task than gleaning potatoes but it was nevertheless a very worthwhile supplement to our pig feed.

By December my saddle-back pig was approaching twenty score (a score was twenty pounds) and again by custom could be killed during any month with the letter r in it. Jim therefore suggested that he should be killed now in October or November, and that I should arrange with Dai Pencae to kill it. Dai lived with his mother in a single-storey shepherd's cottage called Pencae, in the remote Cwm Cyn Nos. He earned his living with the dual occupations of small-holder and pig-killer. I got a message to Dai and it was then arranged that Jim Evans, Dai Pencae and myself should meet in Mrs Griffiths's wash-house, which had formerly been a butcher's shop, the following Friday afternoon at 3.00pm for the actual pig-killing.

On Friday when I arrived the pig was already in the shed, the boiler was lit, the water hot, the bench in position and I was told by Jim, "We've got to get him up on the bench and tie him."

Then began what to me was the most strenuous struggle I had ever been engaged in. With terrified squeals and angry snarls and vicious kicks from the pig, we eventually got him onto his side on the broad low bench. By then my clothes were soaked with urine and manure and there was no way that I could show myself until after dark. I couldn't return to school and Miss Morgan would have to dismiss the children and find her own way home to Llangamarch. The cries of the bound pig were horrendously pitiful and I felt terrified and ashamed of my participation in this orgy of barbaric cruelty.

Dai Pencae was unperturbed. He was a tall, brambly, lean, muscular man, weather-beaten and wearing a brown trilby hat, black serge jacket, cord trousers and hob-nailed boots which emitted a metallic sound as he moved over the stone-flagged floor. He removed a black cloth from his bag and selected a knife. He felt the edge with his thumb, grunted a note of satisfaction and with one deft stroke stuck it into the pig's throat. This increased the pig's screeching and caused me to turn my head away in revulsion. There was an immediate spurt of crimson blood which curled through the air and then gushed from the gaping wound in its throat. The life-blood drained steaming into a bucket placed at the side of the bench. The convulsive shudders ended, the pig finally gasped, exhausted by its struggle to stay alive. It convulsed in a shuddering spasm and died. The coagulated gore clotted on the floor, the steaming blood in the bucket, the blood spattered hands of Dai Pencae, the raw savagery of the occasion were an affront to the dignity of life itself.

The ends of a backset were then forced behind the sinews of the hind legs and the dead pig was hoisted up by a rope slung over a rafter. Using the same knife, the underside was slit from the pubis to the throat and disembowelled into a bath. The rest of the day was spent in washing the intestines, liver, bladder and fats. These different parts were later prepared to make several meat foods such as faggots, brawn and lard. It was the custom at pig-killings to send portions of the meat to friends and relatives, thus ensuring that some fresh meat was made available from September to April to members of an often impoverished community unable to afford this luxury. My pig was conveyed the following day to my home at Cefn Coed where it was cut up into flitches and cured using salt and saltpetre. Meat rationing in 1945 limited families to a small amount of meat weekly, so that a whole pig delivered to the nurse's house was an unprecedented event. I did not, however, ever keep another pig, and the horror of the process of killing animals has stayed with me.

Tennyson's nature "red in tooth and claw" had become a sickening reality to one entirely devoted to the Wordsworthian concept of nature. Daily the sound of silence was punished by the pulsating and anguished cries of trapped, dying or injured creatures. The provenance of this inhumanity lay in ignorance and tradition. The vicious gin-trap-mutilated limbs and on one occasion I was asked to help find a fox which had bitten off its own leg in order to escape. I could accept the falcon or the harrier killing smaller birds as instinctive behaviour in order to survive but the barbarity of pig-killing, the terrible cries, the throat-cutting, the spouting blood, the coagulated clots of purplish blood, I found unbearable. Yet it was witnessed by women and children and has been seen for centuries as a normal part of the farm economy.

An essential part of seasonal life in the Welsh countryside was the movement of cows to farms where there were bulls. Usually the largest farms kept bulls for their own use, the type related to the particular breed that they favoured. If they were interested in meat production they invariably kept Herefords while Friesians were the favourites for milk-production. Payment for bull service was usually by cash but a cottager might pay by labour service at haymaking or harvesting. After the birth of a calf the cow would produce milk and after the calf had been weaned, this milk supply was an important source of income when sold to the Milk Marketing Board or when made into butter or cheese. Surprisingly, it was a traditional farming custom to pay the maid one penny for loosing the bull into the fold on these occasions.

As already stated, a crucial element in the domestic economy was the keeping and killing of pigs. The killing of one, two or three pigs during the winter months followed by salting demanded the services of the local pig-killer, Dai Pencae. The art of salting the pig was usually left to one of the family skilled or interested in this duty. The skill was to prevent the loss of the meat resulting from 'fly blow'. In some parts the flitches and legs were white-limed as an additional precaution. Nothing was wasted. The small meat was shared among neighbours and friends to ensure a meat supply. Since bacon or ham was so important as a home-produced dietary item, boars were necessary to the rural economy. The favourite breeds of pigs at Beulah were large whites which often weighed up to twenty score (400 pounds) and saddlebacks. The piglets were sold locally or taken to the local market at about six weeks old and sold for about six pounds each.

The treatment of sick animals prior to the advent of trained veterinary surgeons was to seek the advice of experienced neighbours, or those in the locality who claimed some special skill. A tape-recording made by Mr Tom Jones of Danydarren, Cwm Taf, for the Welsh Folk Museum, provides fascinating insights into farm life at the turn of this century. He spent the whole of his 88 years on this farm where he was born in 1874 and where he died in 1962.

He refers to well-known sheep complaints and recommends a variety of treatment. These treatments, though primitive and cruel, he claimed were nevertheless successful and variants were dispensed on farms throughout Wales over the years.

For gwaed yn y dwr (blood in the water) some farmers recommended, "Changing the pastures, for foot rot, cut out the infected part and apply Stockholm Tar, or make the sheep walk over burnt lime. For maggots clean out the infected parts and apply oil." Some also recommended putting "saltpetre or tobacco-laden spittle into the eyes of sheep to give them a healthy appearance prior to taking them to market." For constipation or blockage in cows, most efficacious was "tea grounds or hot beer every morning."

I spoke to one shepherd who favoured close-haired dogs working in pairs, one for coursing and one for collecting. He recalled purchasing a pair of good dogs for a pound. A trained dog today can cost up to five hundred pounds. He recalled training dogs and as he stated the golden rule was to wait until the dog was "ready". This was indicated when the dog started chasing chickens around the farm fold. Training proper began with two sheep on the farm fold and much of the training came incidentally by learning from older dogs. He mentioned the problem of killer dogs and pointed out that they never attacked their own flocks but would occasionally work in pairs, killing on other farms.

Referring to traditional methods of stopping a dog from barking while working sheep this old shepherd recommended slitting the dog's tongue or of tying a cork on the tongue. When a sheep dog rushed at the sheep it was useful to tie one foreleg up to its neck and where a dog disobeyed, rhoi leriad iddo fe (give him a good hiding). He claimed that a good dog would be rounding up sheep on the yard in three months and working on its own in ten.

Sheep were 'marked' by cutting a particular pattern in their ears when they were lambs. This was usually done using a shearing scissors or a patented clipper for making round holes in the ear. An additional form of marking was to use an iron and hot pitch. He suggested that the best sheep mark was to sear or burn a mark on the sheep's nose and then rub in fat.

Another farmer described methods of castration used in Breconshire, involving the use of a hot searing iron heated in a wood fire because a coal fire was too hot. He described a method using two pegs tied with hemp and beeswax. Presumably, this method was to restrict the blood supply and was used because it was effective. He and others have confirmed that farmers castrated lambs using their teeth (even in this century. He also mentioned that after marking and castration the male lambs were taken up onto the hill in May.

Boxing Day or St. Stephen's Day was in some parts of Wales commemorated by 'holly beating' of female domestics by men and boys until their arms bled. In the Gower, this was known as 'holming'. This custom has been explained as commemorating the death of St Stephen, while an alternative explanation suggests that 'holming' was associated with the widespread practice of bleeding animals, especially horses, on this day. This periodical bleeding of livestock was believed to be good for the health and staying power of horses and other animals doing hard work. The evidence points to a commemorative ritual supported by primitive medical and veterinary practice as a probable explanation of this custom.

My researches into the Census returns of the Brecon parishes for the nineteenth century revealed some interesting occupations. In the urban parishes along the southern border of Breconshire one notes industrial occupations such as 'sinker', 'cinder carrier' and 'stone breaker', while in the northern parishes 'fox breeder, mole catcher, pig killer and castrator.' Presumably the fox breeder was paid by the local hunts to breed foxes and release them for sport. Mole-catchers at Beulah would usually employ the traditional mole-traps while others would resort to the wooden bridge with a trap door and bucket underneath used in ditches, or even placing a sprig of hawthorn in the mole hill or mole tunnel. The belief in the case of the latter was that a scratch from the thorn would cause a fatal infection for the mole. A modern method of killing moles is by introducing worms dipped in a poison such as arsenic into the mole runs. I have already referred to Dai Pencae, who was the pig-killer for the Beulah area. He was one of the last pig-killers in Wales because very few farmers now keep pigs for domestic consumption and new European regulations no longer permit this method of killing.

The castrator was concerned with the castration of male lambs, bullocks and horses. For centuries bullocks were castrated and used as oxen or fattened and sold to butchers in the local fairs and marts. Bullocks were castrated in the Autumn, 'before the hoar frost.' Oxen have been employed as beasts of burden for centuries, often in teams of eight and exhorted to work by young maidens singing Welsh ditties or traditional songs. One such song said:

> Mu fuo i lawar blwyddyn
> Yn canu gyta'r ychin
> Bara haidd a chosyn cnep
> Dim tishan lap, na phwtin,
> Ma hw, Ma hw.

Translated it reads as follows:
> "For many years
> I sang with the oxen
> Barley bread and lump of cheese
> No cake, no pudding
> Ma hw, Ma hw."

Of interest is the fact that long before the arrival of the Romans the Celts possessed small, rather weak, oxen of around forty inches in height. It was the Romans who introduced the practice of shoeing working oxen with two crescent-shaped pieces of iron on each foot. The plough team varied from six, eight or even twelve oxen yoked in pairs. The yoke was a thick bar of oak or hornbeam carved, polished and oiled. In medieval law a fully grown ox was valued at five shillings; it was yoked to the plough team at three years of age and then worked for six or seven years.

Horses were regarded until the mid-eighteenth century as too noble to undertake the drudgery of ploughing. At this time a controversy arose as to which animal the horse or the ox was most suitable for ploughing and which were the cheaper to keep. From the evidence it would appear that the ox was cheaper to keep for many reasons. After its working life was over it could be killed for meat, its skin could be used for leather and its horns furnished handles, combs and spoons. However, by the last decade of the nineteenth century ox-teams had disappeared in Wales.

The horse was the first animal to benefit from the premiums offered by the Brecknockshire Agricultural Society established in

1755. These premiums were given from 1789, and helped to set in motion the better breeding of horses, for example, "a premium of 20 guineas shall be given for the best stallion, not under four and not more than six years old capable of carrying 16 stone in the field." Then in 1810, a premium of thirty guineas was offered for "the best Suffolk Punch stallion," and "10 guineas for the second best Draught Stallion." Later, premiums were given for horse-breaking and for the shoeing of horses. As a result of this encouragement from the burgeoning Agricultural Societies and Shows, the laying down of hedges for fields and selective breeding produced fine examples of different breeds of horses to fulfil specific needs as farm animals as hunters or ponies. Stallions travelled around between counties and were advertised in the press and by public posters. Some wags claimed that the men who travelled around with the stallions from one farm to another left as many babies behind as the stallions left colts!

Urbanization and the greater use of horses as draught animals in towns and for farm work meant that male horses needed to be castrated at about two years of age or additionally when they were unsuitable for stud. Throughout the nineteenth century horses became immensely important in the mines and iron-works of South Wales and horse-dealers travelled in the Welsh countryside buying horses specifically suitable for these industries. Geldings or castrated stallions and mares purchased even as far afield as Caernarfon were walked back to South Wales in the early decades of this century by well-known and respected horse dealers, such as Tom Kendal of Merthyr. Horse fairs at places like Llanybydder, Lampeter and Llangamarch were well-established centres for the buying and selling of horses. The popularity of the horse as a draught animal continued until the advent of the petrol-driven combustion engine around 1912 and later the tractor after the Second World War.

My arrival at Beulah in 1945 coincided with the demise of the travelling stallion due to increasing use of the tractor and with the growing use of the veterinary service, which was gradually replacing the old traditional animal remedies and the use of pig-killers and castrators. I was suddenly confronted with this hitherto unknown aspect of folk life, which had persisted in Wales for hundreds of years, when I called at the Vicarage to collect my weekly allocation of eggs in the Autumn of 1947. I always left there for the adjacent Aberannell farm to receive my two pounds or so of farm butter and as I left on this night Mrs Hawkins said, "There's a problem over in the farm. You might not find anyone in the kitchen. Something to do with the stallion, so go to the stable. I think they'll be there."

I gently tapped the kitchen door and after a few moments it was opened by Mrs Edwards. Her face expressed her obvious anxiety and before I could ask any questions and, probably, to save any embarrassing questions from me and equally difficult explanations on her part, she said, "The men are over in the stable waiting for the vet." Without asking anything further I walked over the uneven yard towards the half-open stable door. As I slowly entered a lantern hanging from the wall half-illuminated the large stable. I could faintly discern Mr Edwards and his two sons staring at their shire stallion standing forlornly with drooped head and quieter. Normally he would have turned at my entry, and would have been moving his head as if beckoning me into the stable. I sensed something wrong. "What's wrong, Mr Edwards?" I asked.

"Oh," he replied with some feeling in his voice, "I'm afraid we're going to lose him if the vet doesn't come before long."

"How's that?" I queried.

"Well, the gypsy tried to castrate him this afternoon. Something's gone wrong and he's bleeding to death. Look at his leg." He pointed to the far side hind-leg and there was a wide track of blood streaming down it, over the massive hoof, onto the stable floor.

"Only the vet can save him now," said Tom Edwards. "He's got to stop that flow of blood. He's getting weaker." Tom turned to me as his father walked out of the stable. "I warned him not to get the gypsy," he said. "This horse is seventeen hands and worth a lot of money and was earning us a lot of money, but after my accident I couldn't take him around the farms and we decided to sell him as a gelding to the horse dealer from South Wales who came here last week."

Mr Edwards returned. "There's a car coming up the lane," he said. "Let's hope it's the vet. I'll go out and see." With that he left and returned a few minutes later with a stranger, a short, red-faced man dressed in a grey suit of Harris tweed. "Well, what's happened here?" he said, as he bent under the stallion to examine him. After a close examination with his torch he straightened up and, turning to Mr Edwards, angrily exclaimed, "Good Lord, man, why on earth did you let an unqualified potcher mess about with such a valuable horse?" "He's always done these jobs for us without any trouble before," replied a dejected Mr Edwards.

"Well, I don't know whether I can save him. He's lost a lot of blood. The only thing I can do now is to try and stop the bleeding," he added.

With that he opened his leather bag, removed a syringe, filled it and, turning to me, said, "Bring the lantern over here for me to see what I'm doing." He then inserted the syringe into the stallion's neck and started to compress the contents into the animal. Suddenly it reared, gave a ferocious roar and plunged its head downward. This tore the syringe out of the vet's hand as the dying horse kicked both rear legs into the stable wall. Sparks flew from the iron-clad hoofs as it tore at the bridle attached to the manger. Everyone ran for the door as we realized the danger from this crazed monster weighing well over a ton, as it lunged, kicked and snorted in this confined, dimly lit space.

Outside the vet was breathing heavily and by now extremely irritated by the fact that he had risked his life trying to repair the damage done by the "unqualified potcher."

"You know, Edwards," he said, "that horse is going to die because your pal has severed an artery. I'll come back first thing in the morning and if he's still alive I'll have another go."

We parted company in the fold, the vet going to his car and I excusing myself by saying, "I hope things will be alright tomorrow, Mr Edwards, and in any case perhaps the bleeding will stop."

"I don't think there's much chance of that," he said. "He's bled too much, he'll probably be gone by morning." I bade them goodnight and left Aberannell glad to get away from this uncommon and nauseating experience of yet another aspect of rural life. I realized as I walked down the lane that the vet's intention was to render the animal unconscious and then operate on the stable floor. I had been witness to a primitive and traditional form or folk medicine or surgery which had been practised for hundreds of years and in this case had failed. The incident was probably a turning point from an age-old custom to the more scientific approach of the trained veterinary surgeon. The vet returned the following morning. The stallion, still alive, was led out into the fold for a second attempt to stem the haemorrhage. Again he was injected but the result was fatal. He reared up, pawed the morning air, collapsed and died. The Aberannell family were obviously upset by the loss of this fine animal and by the loss of income, but accepted it philosophically as one of those things you can expect in farming. It was just one of the hazards of the job.

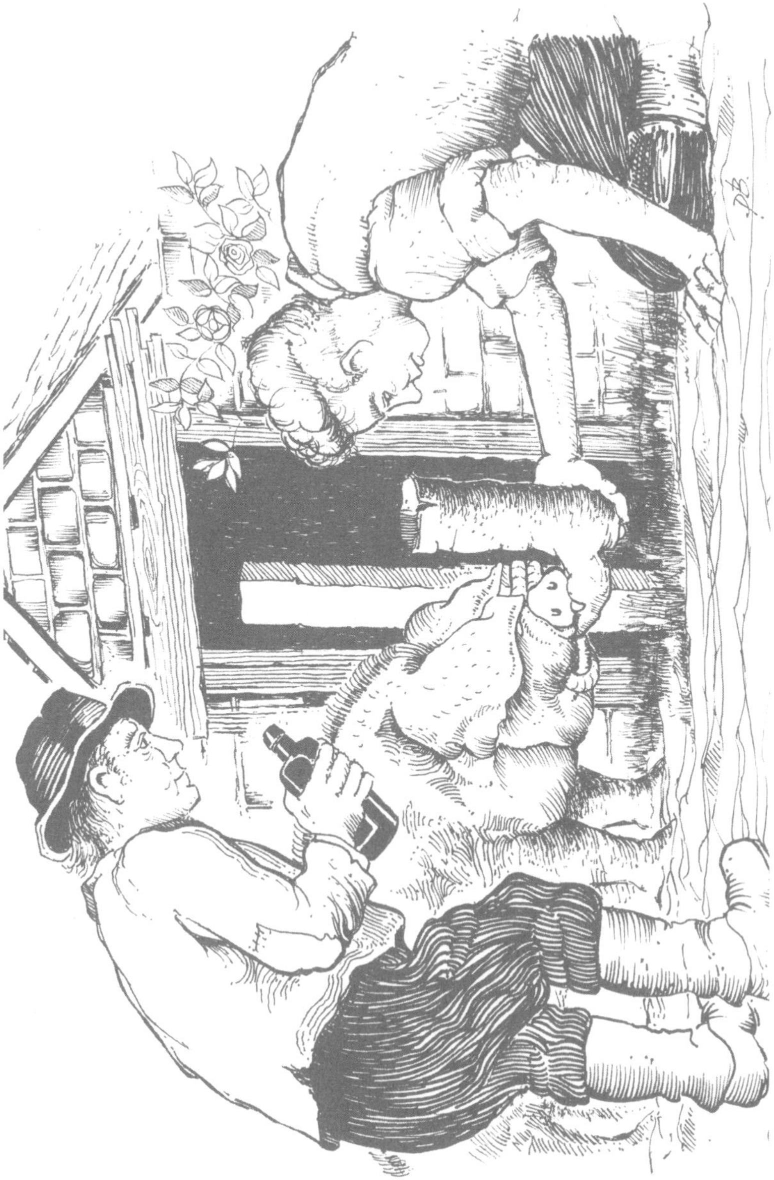

Rural Poverty and some Good Advice

BEING A HEADMASTER AT twenty-two presented far more difficulties than I had ever imagined. There was the overall problem of personal assimilation into a rural culture, involving a new language and social values, trying to teach the age-range from seven to fourteen years in the same classroom and coping with the capitation allowance to cover books and materials on fourteen pounds per annum. Added to this was my total inexperience and incompetence, which made me fearful and overwhelmed as I tried to analyze, for example, the Mathematics and English required for the eleven-plus examination. Furthermore, many children had learning difficulties in reading, writing and mathematics. I felt helplessly stifled and frustrated by so many difficult problems.

The last thing in the world that I wanted at this time was involvement in any controversy or disagreement which would, perhaps, highlight my incompetence in the educational field. However, within weeks of my coming to Beulah I was informed that a girl of about thirteen was constantly running away from home, mixing with gypsies at Builth some fourteen miles away and was generally a problem. She was tall, slimly built, pretty, poorly dressed and wearing heavily nailed boots. Her threadbare dress and ill-fitting coat suggested domestic poverty and her unkempt hair some degree of deprivation. She and her two cousins were cared for by elderly grandparents.

During one of her frequent absences from school I decided one afternoon to visit her home about two miles from Beulah, in order to explore her social background. With some difficulty I found a roadside gate leading to a single-storeyed cottage with a few adjacent agricultural buildings. I stood on the threshold of the neglected cottage and peered through the open upper half of the door which provided both ventilation and light into the small, dimly lit kitchen. The bare stone-paved floor led towards a white scrubbed table upon which a cockerel was pecking and scratching among the unwashed crockery. Under the table a half-grown pig was grunting and pushing a white enamel bowl about, which had probably contained some scraps of food. Directly behind the table was a wood fire which illuminated the sham fireplace, the mantleshelf, and the brown beamed ceiling supporting some flitches of home-cured bacon. My presence soon disturbed two large black and white sheepdogs which barked and snarled as they threw themselves at the closed lower half of the door. This cacophony brought the two adults out of their fireside chairs, shouting at the dogs to cwtch.

A bald man with a few days' stubble, stooping with age dragged his unlaced boots over the uneven floor towards me. He revealed gaunt anxiety in his pale-blue eyes. His open stained waistcoat covered a threadbare, torn, grey jumper and an open- necked, Welsh flannel shirt.

"Good afternoon," he said, "Can I help you?"

"I'm Bowen, the schoolmaster at Beulah," I replied. "Can I have a chat with you, please?"

"Certainly, come on in," he answered. With that he unbarred the lower half of the door.

"Cwtch, cwtch," he shouted to the dogs, which slunk growling into the shadows.

"Sit by the fire, Mr Bowen," said the old lady. "We're glad to see you, because we're very worried about our granddaughter. I sat in the fireside chair while the protesting pig and cockerel were ushered out of the impoverished kitchen and into the dung-covered yard outside. I waited until both the old people were seated before I explained my mission, which was to report that their granddaughter was absent from school, and to discuss with them the danger of her Saturday visits to the gypsy encampment at Builth.

The old man nodded his agreement and added, "We really don't know what we can do about it. She runs away under our noses and we have no means of catching her."

"The truth is, Mr Bowen, we are too old to look after them. My husband is a shepherd for a number of farmers and is away on the hill from early in the morning and we just can't watch her," mumbled the stroke-impaired woman.

I gazed into her wan, wizened, wrinkled countenance. Her body was enfeebled by unremitting toil and age, innocent of the ways of the world and unable to cope with this extra burden. The unyielding soil, inclement weather and isolation on a rock-strewn smallholding in upland Wales had little to commend it. This was a miserable, frightening picture of poverty and despair which I thought only existed in the industrial slums of South Wales. Rural poverty, if anything, was worse than living in the congested rat-infested slums of South Wales where it was a shared communal problem of poverty and squalor, as opposed to the soul-searing pain of isolation. How different was this agonizing weariness, fatigue and sadness compared with the delectable food, animation and enchantment of the Hunt Ball at Llanwrtyd some weeks previously!

"My wife's suffered a stroke and that's why I'm here today, to carry the water from the well and to help around the house," said the old man. The sagging eye, the drooping jaw and her almost incoherent speech confirmed this debilitating condition. Her fearful eyes expressed her intense anxiety, her frail lop-sided posture clearly indicated a fatal illness. The cumulative effect of poverty, ill health and old age was inextricably entwined with the added burden of caring for three grandchildren in a hostile environment. This was the reality of country life, where all human endeavours took place against the non-human background of bare bleak hills, deep wooded valleys varied and beautiful, which provide their opportunities for work and for all they can accomplish by way of self-fulfilment. My pre-conception of rural life was ill-founded. How on earth did the peasantry exist and survive the rigours of rural life over the centuries in damp thatched cottages, isolation, poverty and disease?

I gazed with sorrow into the honest, inquiring face, imagining her in her youth, with classical features, a graceful and slender body combined with dignity and sweetness. Beneath lay a charming and simple personality, but now her illness made her smile waver on her wrinkled cheeks, giving her a distorted countenance that begged compassion. She appeared to have a psychic blindness: she was seeing me without fully comprehending. In contrast, how beautiful it was outside where the song of the thrush was disturbed only by the warm breeze blowing over the dew-glistening meadows. What a paradox life is when one reflects upon the enchanting loveliness of the May countryside, with the absence of apparent evil influence and the peace and tranquillity of this place, were it not for the grinding poverty and terrors of age and circumstance.

"She's absent from school today, is she, Mr Bowen?" asked the old man.

"What did the other children say, has she gone to Builth? We are getting a lot of trouble," he added. "What with her running away and staying out at night. We don't really know what to do with her." His tone signified despondency and hopelessness.

"Can you do something for to help?" mumbled the grandmother.

I gazed at the brass-hinged, well-thumbed Bible lying on the black, round table in the corner. A silver-framed picture of two laughing girls stood askew on the Bible. "Those are our daughters," said the old man. "Both are away working in England."

"How often do you see them?" I asked.

"Not very often," stammered the old lady. "You see, they have young families of their own now and can't get down here to see us. They can't afford to."

The dark kitchen exuded so much sadness and deep gloom that it pervaded every corner, and moved me to say that I would report their circumstances to the Chief Education Officer, and that I was sure he would be able to help them. I stepped off the threshold into a bed of mud and manure, inhabited by sallow-faced calves, geese, ducks and newly shorn sheep.

"Perhaps we'd better let the police know that she's missing?" I suggested to the old shepherd.

"I'll do that and I'll let the Education Authorities know too. They'll help you," I said. "Thank you, Mr Bowen," he responded. "I don't want her to get into trouble, I do appreciate what you are trying to do for us, but can you see my circumstances? Really, I shouldn't leave my wife, but I am a communal shepherd and I should be up on the hill every day or I'll lose my job."

"Don't worry now," I said, "she'll come home tonight and I'll have a chat with her and get Nurse Davies to speak to her as well." He lifted his hand as a token of thanks and nodded his head as if he realized, too, that the situation was hopeless.

I passed through the crowd of pecking hens, gabbling geese and the gander who hissed his displeasure with outstretched neck and flapping wings as he went for my legs. I strutted sombrely along the deep-rutted roadway, hastening away, escaping from my rendez-vous with rural poverty and squalor.

I again, immediately, reported the case to the Director of Education with the additional information of the home circumstances of the family. I expressed my deep concern regarding her running away from home and that she was apparently sleeping in barns and associating with the Builth gypsies.

I received no acknowledgement, but when I arrived at school the following Monday at 8.45am I recognized the Director's car parked in the yard. As I entered the school the caretaker, Mrs Evans greeted me with the confirmation, "There's two gentlemen in there." I nodded and entered the little hall to see the Director and Chief Clerk perusing some letters on the dining-room table. I was invited to sit down on one of the benches and with the full authority at his command the Director stated, "We've come here to tell you that we do not consider that there's anything wrong with this girl, and I would like to warn you that if you pursue your activities with regard to this girl you could appear in court on a charge of libel."

I responded by pointing out that I had acted upon a number of reliable and diverse reports, which indicated that this young girl was 'at risk'. I further explained the dire circumstances of her aged grandparents, but to no avail. I was amazed that a man who himself had once been breaking rocks in the Welsh quarries and who had known deprivation in his younger days could now exhibit such frightening disregard for this delinquent girl. My protest that it was illogical and tragic to ignore the warnings was met with total intransigence. He left in a sombre mood and that was our last verbal encounter for some years. When I arrived at my lodgings that afternoon, I was confronted by a young policeman, later to become a Chief Constable, who informed me that the girl had been found living on a remote farm in the Abergwesyn area.

During the following morning Nurse Davies arrived at school. "I've not come to do the inspection, Mr Bowen," she said, "but to report that M .... J.... has been selling brand new pairs of shoes around the village."

"Where's she getting them from?" I asked.

"I understand she's getting them from Jim Eadie's shop in Builth," she replied.

Jim Eadie, whom I had never met, was a celebrated and respected Breconshire County Councillor for Builth and Chairman of the Education Committee. I immediately responded by saying, "I'll go down and see him tonight to establish where she's getting these shoes from." By 4.30 pm I had found out from Councillor Eadie how she had obtained so many pairs of new shoes from his shop. Her grandfather, a communal shepherd, was paid annually and once a year he paid his bills for any shoes purchased at Mr Eadie's shop. This girl had simply purchased a dozen or so pairs of shoes on his account and then re-sold them locally at Beulah.

"You'd better go across the road and check them out as well," he said, "because as a family they deal there too." He was referring to a general outfitters shop and when I enquired, I was informed that she had indeed, by the same pretext, obtained a number of 'new look' coats and dresses which she had probably also sold.

There was hardly any need for me to catalogue my failure to convince the Chief Education Officer of this girl's exploits and of her personal circumstances. "You just leave this to me," said Mr Eadie with a grim smile. "I'll sort this lot out, don't you worry."

While there was now a glimmer of hope that something might be done to avert disaster for this young delinquent, I still found the languor, the quiescence and professional neglect suffocating. In this frame of mind I made tentative arrangements with the Director of Education for the Army Northern Command, to rejoin the army as a lieutenant in the Education Corps. However, when I returned to school on the following Monday, my caretaker informed me that the girl had been arrested over the weekend for stealing bicycles and repainting them prior to reselling them. Thus my efforts to save her from such a situation were in vain. She was subsequently tried in the Builth juvenile court and placed in a special school for three years. Some years after leaving Beulah, I heard she had married and died young. She exemplified tragically so many children unhappily introduced into a harsh world and into a particular set of adverse circumstances which predetermine their lives of misery and pain.

The maxim, 'You cannot put an old head on young shoulders,' was certainly true when I reflect upon my inexperience and inability to judge wisely, due primarily to my naïve principles stemming from a working-class background and reinforced, I suppose, by my genetic inheritance. I had, too, a rebellious streak confirming my descent, I suppose, from Dafydd Lewis, one of the Unitarian leaders of the Merthyr Rising of 1831. This almost puritanical zeal to right the world's wrongs provoked a breach in my relationship with my superior, over what I considered then to be a failure on his part to help a delinquent child, a child who was deprived, a victim of rural poverty and ignorance.

My futile attempts to save this child seemed to be blocked by bureaucracy and disregard. Her behaviour worsened and my protests were interpreted as biased and libellous, until by a strange set of circumstances my fears were confirmed and she was taken into care. This train of disastrous events, I felt, could have been avoided by a judicious intervention by the official concerned and I aired this view. Professionally, I had committed a cardinal sin; I was now out of favour, isolated to rot in the countryside. I was soon made to realize that recalcitrance would not enhance my position. I was left to the long winters of cold nights, deep snow and lonely hours to speculate upon my future, a sadder but wiser man.

The new Director of Education was a formidable character who had risen from a quarryman to the rank of Air Commodore during the recent war and latterly to be Chief Education Officer. He soon indicated his undoubted ability by organizing week-long courses for all primary teachers, held twice yearly at Brecon. These courses were highly successful because they involved the best tutors available, field trips and relevant books on the current historical and educational topics. One of these courses, 'The Welsh Methodists', was to break my Nonconformist isolation in my dealings with my contemporaries - especially with my superiors. At least, I thought so then, but in fact, my general tendency has been over the years to resist injustice, to care for the weak and not worry too much about the consequences.

We congregated for the buses at Brecon, some two hundred teachers covering the human spectrum of age, sex, appearance and ambition. Some wore tweeds, coats and hats reflecting individual tastes, status and discernment. They were a motley host of dedicated souls, led by broad-shouldered, Welsh-speaking, benevolently smiling and nodding Deiniol Williams, the Chief Education Officer. His suit was of thick, drab, cheerless, hard-wearing Welsh tweed reflecting the wearer's personality in every visible respect. Buses arrived and with chuckles, polite gestures and smiles the convoy of teachers disappeared en route for the home of Howell Harris at Trefeca.

After a lecture in Trefeca Chapel, and a visit to the Trefeca Museum, we departed and some distance from Llangeitho, the shrine of Daniel Rowland, we stopped and walked along a lane sheltered by thick hedgerows alive with captivating birdsong, affirming the glory of Maytime. The disorderly crowd, in twos and threes, happily enjoying respite from the unending classroom toil, moved slowly towards the houses indicated by ascending swirls of smoke, bluish grey roofs, a chapel and some distance in the foreground our destination, the church at Llangeitho, associated with the great Methodist, Daniel Roland.

As we walked along the winding, flower-banked lane I heard Deiniol Williams, the Chief Education Officer, calling "Bowen, could I have a word with you?" I turned with much surprise to find him at my side.

"Listen, Bowen," he said. "You're an able schoolmaster but you are fast becoming the stormy petrel of this County. Do you know what a stormy petrel is?"

"I think it's a bird," I replied.

"Yes, quite correct," he said. "It's a bird that flies against the wind. You are like that bird, Bowen, and let me tell you something else. You will fly further, and much faster, if you fly with the wind."

I looked at him and realized that he was giving me good advice. I said, "That seems to be good advice, thank you, Mr Williams."

"Alright, now I want you, as the Senior Headmaster here today, to do two things. First of all, I want you to look after that man with the grey tweed suit standing by the gate, and I would like you to thank the ladies of the Llangeitho Women's Institute for providing us with a meal after our visit to the Church. Will you do those two jobs for me?" he asked.

"Yes, certainly," I replied without asking who the gentleman was and what I was supposed to do. This stranger was in animated conversation with a group of teachers and so I decided to be as unobtrusive as possible, but would sit by him in church, if I had the opportunity to do so. I wondered who this stranger was and how he came to be with us. Nevertheless, I was glad that Deiniol Williams and I were now friends and that I was now out of the wilderness of isolation created by my inexperience in dealing with what I considered to be an injustice. I obviously had a lot to learn with regard to relating my principles to my superiors. I shudder at my effrontery in dealing with this man who had risen from cutting rock in the Welsh quarries to become an Air Commodore sending hundreds of bombers nightly to bomb industrial centres, gun emplacements and aerodromes in Germany. The analogy to the stormy petrel flying against the wind was obvious. "Henceforth I shall fly with the wind," I said to myself.

The animated chattering of the gathering crowd of teachers around the lychgate of Llangeitho Church dissipated as we reverently greeted the dark flashing eyes and the serious welcome of the parish priest. We filed ghost-like along the aisles. I sat in the front seat with my unknown guest whom I had been told to look after. I wondered whether this was the church which Daniel Rowland had known and loved, whether the architecture, the altar lit by the cascading sunbeams pouring forth from the stained-glass windows, the oak-lidded font and the rows of pitch-pine pews were those revered by Rowland. It was in this reflective mood that I breathed the eloquence of sacred light and silence, and I was mindful of Henry Vaughan's poem 'Regeneration', and the lines:

"The unthrift sun shot vital gold
A thousand pieces,
And heaven its azure did unfold
Chequered with snowy fleeces."

The young priest welcomed us to his church and when everyone was seated said, "This is the pulpit used by Daniel Rowland." Every eye turned to the oak pulpit, but I detected a slight shake of the head from my guest sitting at my side. The vicar repeated his statement considerably louder and with a frowning emphasis directed in my direction. My guest responded with a formal disagreeing shake of his head, which evoked a sullen scream from the vicar, "This is Daniel Rowland's pulpit, and I've noticed you disagreeing with me three times," he said, pointing to my friend. My guest responded by stating, "If you turn to page ... in a book entitled ... in the National Library you will find a photograph of Daniel Rowland's pulpit with 'D.R.' carved on it." Within the church one now sensed a tension totally inappropriate to the point of indecency. The vicar's anger and frustration exploded as he pointed to the door and shouted "Get out, the lot of you!"

With goggle-eyed amazement, the congregation, which only seconds before had been bowing before the altar, praying or gazing in silence at the artefacts within the church, were unceremoniously ejected and rudely consigned to the gathering clouds, the spring flowers amid the graves and inscribed slabs bedded in ivy, nettles and grass. I followed my guest out, floundering in a mixture of dismay, disgust and amusement at this immoderate and unnecessary circumstance arising from such a triviality. Not so, however, with the vicar who approached us in a perceptibly angry mood. An imperious question was thrown at us from some yards distant. "Who should know?" he bellowed.

"I should," replied my unruffled companion.

"How should you know?" he countered.

"Look, my good fellow," my companion replied, "do you see that white farmhouse on the hill? Well, seven generations of my family have lived there and worshipped at this church – as I did as a boy."

"Oh yes," said the vicar, displaying now a more visibly deferential tone. After a pause he turned again to my friend and, with a puzzled look, said, "Well, who are you?"

"In answer to that question," my friend modestly replied, "I attended that little school, from there I went to the local Secondary School, from there to Oxford."

"You've not told me who you are," said the vicar.

"I am Evan Jones, Keeper of Manuscripts at the National Library of Wales, Aberystwyth," he replied in a clear voice. The vicar, with frenzied look and facial shades of green masking his tortured embarrassment, fidgeted for a moment in despair, as he gathered that the murmurs of ridicule and shrieks of laughter were directed towards him. He turned, tried to weave between the tombs and the amazed, silent groups of teachers pondering on this most ill-tempered and ill-judged action of the vicar who then loudly shouted, "You've only come here today to cause trouble between the Methodists and the Church."

My guest then replied, "Don't be ridiculous, vicar," but by then the cleric had disappeared among the stones.

While the disagreement proceeded, I was in a quandary as to what I should say and do, in view of the fact that Deiniol had likened me to a stormy petrel. Did he think I had anything to do with this débâcle? I was acutely aware that he was staring at me both in the Church and now in the graveyard. For a moment our eyes met and he beckoned me across to him. He led me away from the others.

"Bowen," he said, "you've learnt your second lesson today. Never underestimate your audience or, for that matter, don't underestimate anyone." He looked at me with a perceptive eye and I knew exactly what he meant .... "Don't underestimate me either, Bowen bach."

The Eisteddfod and the Hunt Ball

IT WAS DURING MY early days in the village that I first heard of the Beulah Eisteddfod and the Beulah Show. While the latter caused me little surprise because it was an agricultural area and I imagined a small local show, I was exceedingly surprised to hear that the Eisteddfod was an annual event which had gone on for many years. Furthermore, there were also annual Eisteddfodau held at nearby Llangamarch and Llanwrtyd. My surprise was really a reflection of my ignorance of the cultural life of rural Wales and its traditions. That a small hamlet set in the heartland of mid-Wales, surrounded by awesomely majestic scenery of tree-clad hills and hidden valleys dotted with isolated farms and a landscape of wild moorland, would have the population, interest and literary and musical knowledge to consider holding an Eisteddfod amazed me. In saying this I should add that my personal knowledge of Eisteddfodau was limited to the School Eisteddfodau of my old Grammar School at Cefn Coed.

I was invited to the first meeting of the Eisteddfod Committee in the Spring of 1946 at seven o'clock in the village hall. This was a small building located at the side of the main road between the Carpenters' Arms and Nurse Davies's house. Soon the members started arriving: Mr Alfred Jones, bespectacled, studious and serious, was the first. He represented a host of natural scholars denied the chance of Grammar School education and college through circumstances of impoverishment or large families. Then came Elvet Powell, owner of Maesllech farm, tall, handsome, witty and independent of the Llwyn Madoc estate because of his freeholder status. Then came Cyril Price, Cyril had attended Builth Grammar School, had been in the army with me and was now the local undertaker and carpenter. Then came Bill Cobbler, the Secretary, Vicar Brynley Hawkins, the nurse, Charlie Smith, gardener on the Estate, and Gib Lewis, farmer and basket-maker. Later came many others, ruddy-faced and dressed in homespun tweed, and thick black boots and smiling to their many friends.

Although they had walked along roads, rugged mountain paths and winding lanes from upland isolated farms in the neighbouring parishes, they represented a community of people with close ties of kinship, language, religion and culture. Community meant more than just a group of people living in the village. This sense of unity was evident in the animated greetings both in English and Welsh, when they asked about families and friends in Abergwesyn, Garth or Llanafan Fawr. They had been in school together, attended the same chapel, married into the same families, bought and sold animals to one another, attended the marts and markets together and knew one another and their reputations well. This knowledge of one another, which included their characters, morality, financial status and so on, was important especially when their children started courting. Where the respective families were of good character, honest and of equal status financially, so that both families could provide for the young couple to set up a farm, they received the blessing of the parents. However, a farmer's son was not encouraged to marry a girl out of farming, for example, a labourer's daughter or teacher who might not be able to enter into the marriage with a dowry.

Upon entering the hall each individual addressed everyone with a general "Hello all," and then joined one or other of the groups standing around discussing the mart prices at Builth, pigs, the Black Market and general news. Eventually, the Chairman called them together to discuss the business of the Eisteddfod. After a financial report from the Treasurer, the real business of the evening began. They discussed the venue, date, the various items for literary and musical competitions in English and Welsh. Finally, a decision was made that Crwys, the crowned bard, should be the literary adjudicator, and W.S. Parry, the Cefn Coed composer, the music adjudicator. These were unanimously passed and recorded by Bill Cobbler, the Eisteddfod secretary in English.

I listened astounded at the individual and collective knowledge of Welsh and English literature, the relevant qualities of the poems, their suitability for various age groups and the dates when and where these items had been used in Beulah or other local Eisteddfodau. This applied equally to the musical items, when detailed discussions took place over tenor solos or soprano pieces that I had never heard of. They even discussed the themes for poems and hymn-tunes to be composed by certain dates and the merits of poets and composers both national and local. I was left humbled by this profound demonstration of Welsh culture.

Upon reflection some fifty years later, I now realize that this knowledge, interest and culture were derived from the chapel culture which had dominated Welsh society in the nineteenth century and that its influence was still apparent in the mid-twentieth. The Nonconformist Chapel embodied the Protestant individualism that has influenced so many Welsh people. The independence of the chapel attracted people anxious to throw off the shackles of authoritarianism in the mining districts or the squire in the rural areas. The chapel was looked upon as a civilizing influence; it represented not only a gospel of salvation for the individual but a whole way of life mainly based on the Welsh language. This in turn was identified with Eisteddfodau, the Cymanfa Ganu, the Band of Hope, the Temperance movement, radical politics, the Sunday School movement, Education and the Welsh literary and musical tradition. I was witnessing a voluntary group demonstrating clearly their traditional affinity with Nonconformity in a viable Welsh-language heartland, y fro Gymraeg, through the medium of the local Eisteddfod which had been the breeding ground of local poets and scholars.

Meetings were held regularly when amendments were made to the proposed programme, letters were read, reports made and everyone within the context of this rural community reflected a sense of responsibility and cultural identity. The success of the Eisteddfod was obviously a concern of the community. It perpetuated an essential element in the tapestry of Welshness and the Nonconformist ethos. I was made acutely aware that I was having a retrospective glimpse of past meetings held in farmhouse kitchens and inns decades or even centuries ago, to organize the building of chapels, to plan Eisteddfodau or riots. I was introduced to the riches of another and older culture which had virtually disappeared from the urban area where I had been nurtured.

The Eisteddfod day on the last Saturday in May dawned with a coppery sky, caught in the belt of cloud hovering in the east, and with the voices of early birds brimful of morning songs and delighted with the prospect of a lovely day. The morning sun streamed through the crevices of the white canvas marquee, giving a warm glow to the silent shades of empty chairs, tables, benches and tent poles. The vicarage field, bordered by grass banks, hedges, gnarled elms and ashes clad with new foliage, provided a picturesque rural setting, with the Victorian Vicarage behind the straggling oaks and winding drive. It was grand in its simplicity and the sublimity of the natural beauty surrounding the field was majestic on this May morning. Local weather forecasters referring to ancient phenomena such as sun, moon, stars, clouds, winds, candle flames, swallows, smoke and river mist were unanimous in prophesying a warm, dry day – and how right they were.

By midday the farmers were hanging up their scythes, reaping hooks, ropes and harness, putting away the gambos, carts and wheelbarrows. Thick black whiskers were torn from their red faces, cords were replaced by Sunday tweeds, heavy boots by black shoes, torn caps by bowlers or trilbies, flannel shirts by white collars and ties. Upstairs, children and mothers were likewise engaged in adorning themselves with best clothes, summer dresses, grey suits and colourful ribbons. The stock had been fed, gates secured, doors locked, fires extinguished, money hidden, tables cleared, watches wound, hair combed and beribboned prior to the last glance round the kitchen for the programmes, competition pieces, the gloves and hats and keys.

By two o'clock the ticket attendants at the Lodge gate were already busy greeting old faces, making innocent jokes, collecting entrance fees, offering advice and sitting and standing under the withered oaks, gaunt with age and storms. Occasionally, they doffed their bowlers and smiled in deference to some fashionably dressed lady or acclaimed poet or musician. While wealth provided status and power, poetic skill proven by winning cups, crowns and chairs or great musical talent also afforded status and prestige. These were the descendants of the old bardic order, the sagas and men of wisdom and scholarship entitled as of old to the respect of their contemporaries. Poor men of humble birth could thus, through their native talents, slowly rise to an almost mystical position of eminence in local peasant life or even have national recognition through the Eisteddfod. Miners, colliers, ironworkers, farm servants, farmers, blacksmiths, weavers and wheelwrights arrived to witness and compete. Success would later be recalled with pride by children and grandchildren, cups would be polished and exhibited, treasured and honoured in parlours with family Bibles, mahogany chests of drawers, family photographs, round tables, deep-red-cushioned chairs and grand-father clocks.

The Eisteddfod proceedings were conducted by an arweinydd, who generally managed the children's competitions in the afternoon and the adults in the evening session. Conducting an Eisteddfod, lasting in this case for nearly twelve hours in an orderly manner, keeping the audience in good humour with witticisms and humorous stories, was an art in itself. The conductor also had to cope with a few local boys who were heckling, and he used the time-honoured method of dealing with them by ridicule and defeating them in a contest of wit. These small village Eisteddfodau afforded the opportunities for people to speak in public, to perform before an audience, to learn from the adjudicator's criticism and to develop their own critical faculties. Winning at this level provided the encouragement and confidence to compete in county Eisteddfodau and perhaps ultimately in the National Eisteddfod. The adjudicators and the arweinydd could distinguish themselves too in the same way. Achievements at this level were matters of pride for the parishioners, especially when a native became a celebrated poet or musician.

Genial fresh-complexioned boys and prettily dressed girls, some faint-hearted, others brimful of confidence, demure, light-hearted or fidgety, recited or sang their pieces, demonstrating concentration, training, enthusiasm and talent, revealing folk culture at its highest level. The adjudicators awarded prizes for interpretation, intonation, quality of voice and accuracy, which were usually couched in terms of encouragement, acclaiming the competitors for their efforts and advocating certain points for future consideration. Hearty applause was given to the various adjudications, so that even losers and their disappointed teachers and parents were comforted by the intelligent criticism, the congratulations and the prospect of future success.

The adult compositions manifested, as one would expect, a greater degree of competition and concentration upon winning. Some acquitted themselves with abounding talent and smiling countenances, others exerted themselves to the point of exhaustion, grimacing as they left the stage disappointed and saddened by their efforts. Winners were effervescent, translating their success into hugs and tears of joy, while losers appeared despondently affronted and aggravated with themselves and with their adjudicators. The adjudicators listened, scribbled and occasionally nodded in approbation or slowly shook their heads. The more informed among the audience and supporters of the competitors, scrutinized and read the expressions of the adjudicators praying for a nod.

The evening quietude was drowned by the solos, the frenzied applause and the movement of buses bringing choirs from distant places. They congregated in groups, listened intently to last warnings as they solemnly entered the arena and onto the stage. Aladdin lamps provided the illumination, accompanists male and female swept by to the piano, gripped in the solemnity of this finale of weeks of practice. Some of the conductors were as white-headed as snow-capped mountains, others short and important, or bowed in the shoulders under the stress shown by the manic glaze of their serious faces. The ochreous haze of expiring sunlight, and the red glow caught in a belt of cloud, greeted the last competitors as they arrived and prepared for the champion solos and the chief choral competitions for silver cups. By two in the morning the last adjudications were received with groans, sadness or cheers, hand- clapping or sullen silence. The motley crowd, some delighted, others sad, boarded buses or sped away in cars. Many others walked into the darkness, bordered by trees, hedges and other vegetation, along winding lanes and woodland paths. A place of watchful intentness by night, but grand in its sublimity of beauty and simplicity in the morning sun.

The Eisteddfod was acclaimed as an outstanding success in terms of the weather, the large attendance, and the outstanding quality of the competitors. Among those who excelled that afternoon both in elocution and music was a young and exceptionally attractive young lady from Radnorshire, whom I arranged to meet the following Tuesday evening at the Lake Hotel in Llandrindod. During the course of the next few days, I discovered that one of the local boys, Emlyn Price, had relatives at Llandrindod. I suggested that he should come along with me on my motorcycle and visit his family when I was going to meet this young lady, and this he readily accepted. The distance from Beulah was about twenty-four miles so this was very convenient for him.

When we arrived at Llandrindod for some unknown reason I left my motorcycle at Mr Norton's garage instead of a public parking place. This garage in its architecture, position and grandeur, resembled more a palace than a garage. It was in every respect a prestigious business set in the centre of town, while the owner, Mr Tom Norton, was a revered and respected character in Radnorshire and north Breconshire. It was such a grand affair that I was surprised that they allowed a motorcycle anywhere near the premises. However, they did – without informing me that they closed at 9.00pm.

There are occasions when some things go wrong, but this was a night when everything went disastrously so from beginning to end. First was the alarming news from the young lady that she suffered from T.B. I met up with Emlyn outside the Palace about 9.30pm only to find to our dismay, that it was already closed with my motorcycle, our only means of transport home, locked up inside. From the café-owner opposite we elicited the information that Mr Norton resided at the Metropole Hotel, the largest in Llandrindod.

There really was no choice other than to find Mr Norton, and explain my embarrassing situation, and try to retrieve my bike. The hotel porter, gold-braided in a blue uniform, obligingly informed Mr Norton that a gentleman in the foyer wished to speak to him. Within seconds of giving this message the foyer door swung open and the local Inspector of Schools for Breconshire and Radnorshire appeared, carrying tennis racquets and a college coat of many colours.

"Hello, Mr Bowen, come to see me, have you?" he asked.

"No, sir, I'm waiting to retrieve my motorcycle from Mr Norton's garage. It's been inadvertently locked in there," I said. "I'm waiting to see him now."

He looked rather puzzled but said, as Mr Norton shuffled towards us, "I'll call in to see you tomorrow."

"Alright, sir," I muttered, wondering at the same time how I was going to get back to Beulah in time to meet him.

"Are you the gentleman who wanted to meet me?" said a voice suddenly. "I'm Tom Norton, what can I do for you?"

A man of distinguished appearance, grey-haired, bespectacled, serious with a facial expression suggesting a thoughtful man used to deliberating over questions of policy stood before me; indeed, a man who probably had built up a very successful business by care, shrewdness and business acumen.

Taken a little unaware, I spluttered out my predicament, now more concious than ever of my extreme foolishness in what I had done. He looked at me with astonishment, either with my effrontery in coming to the hotel, or at my stupidity in leaving my bike at his garage without checking out details of closure.

"We close at 9.00pm prompt," he growled. "This is extremely

inconvenient for me because I've only just left there, and the hotel staff are now preparing my evening meal."

"I do apologize," I said. "Do you think I could ask someone to open up instead of dragging you down there?"

"There's no one with the keys except me," he said. He hesitated and was obviously considering his next move. He rubbed his chin, glanced sideways at me and then said, "Alright, you go down and I'll follow you."

Twenty minutes later the bike was wheeled out. I thanked him profusely, he smiled and I waved as we sped off down and out of Llandod, as it is known locally. Alas, I immediately discovered that we had a flat tyre, and no puncture outfit and it was getting dark.

"The only thing you can do now," suggested Emlyn, "is pump the tyre up as hard as possible and go as far as we can."

This seemed the only answer and every so often we stopped, pumped away, rode as fast as possible and repeated the process. There seemed no immediate problem as we arrived at the top of the steep hill near the village of Howey, then suddenly there was a most violent explosion from the rear end, the bike wobbled, went totally out of control, turned violently to the right and we shot across the road down an embankment and into a water-filled ditch. The bike spluttered, steamed and stopped. Poor Emlyn stood shaking his hands, wiping his face and looking forlornly at his grey 'de-mob' suit, soaked and shrinking. We had to stand in a foot of brackish water in order to try and drag the bike up the slope to the road.

"We'll have to leave it now," said Emlyn. "Let's try and find a telephone and phone Bill Cobbler to come and get us."

"That's all we can do ," I agreed so we squelched along as the stars began to appear, hoping to find a telephone somewhere along the ten miles between Howey and Builth.

Providence was good and after walking about two miles Emlyn spied a light shining dimly from a farmhouse a hundred yards or so from the road.

"Let's go up there," he said, "perhaps they've got a phone."

We opened a latched gate leading up to a square, bay-windowed, old, stone-fronted farmhouse.

I rang the bell and waited. The response was a double-barrelled gun pushed through a side window.

"What do you want?" said a rough female voice from behind the curtains.

The gun pointed ominously at my chest two yards away; at this range she just couldn't miss!

"Could we use your telephone, please, to get some help? We've just crashed on my motorcycle up the road and I need to get back to Beulah tonight if that's possible."

"Who are you?" came a second voice.

"This is my friend and my name is Bowen, I'm the schoolmaster at Beulah." Another long pause ended with the unbolting of the door.

"Only one in," said the voice.

I stepped in after seeking Bill's telephone number from Emlyn. The armed lady prodded me in the back with the barrel of the gun and said, "Follow her," indicating a wizened, lean old lady in her eighties carrying a candle in a brass candlestick. The telephone was placed on an oak coffer in the cold, dimly lit stone-flagged hallway. I phoned, offered money for the call but was escorted to the door and allowed out. "Thank you very much," I called but the door slammed, the sleeping dogs were awakened and we ran down to the road hotly pursued by two sheepdogs.

We were nearing Builth by the time Bill arrived in his 1930 two-seater Austin Seven. I reached Beulah about one in the morning to find that Miss Parry had locked the door. Using the ivy, I managed to climb the drainpipe and into my bedroom without too much bother. The H.M.I. arrived the following morning and that night, ably helped by Emlyn and Bill Cobbler, I replaced the torn tyre, repaired the puncture using Bill's repair outfit and foot-pump because mine had disappeared. However, upon reflection it might still be lying in that water-filled ditch at Howey. I was glad that there would not be another Eisteddfod at Beulah for another year!

The Welsh countryside with entirely new and different values, customs and traditions stripped away almost all recreational activities. Any leisure activities were therefore limited to walking to Garth, Llanafan or Abergwesyn or riding my motorcycle at speed along the narrow country roads. Danny Davies, teaching at Llanwrtyd, occasionally called for me and I drove his car to Llandrindod or I visited his home Bryn Irfon, a lovely hotel run by his sister at nearby Llanwrtyd.

It was on one of these rare outings to Llanwrtyd that I became totally bewitched by a young lady of exquisite beauty. Her raven-black hair matched her olive skin and deep set laughing eyes, radiating intelligence and joy. Her laughter rang with merriment, her cherry lips revealed her pearly white teeth flashing and making her finely shaped features more appealing and enchanting. Her trim, tall and statuesque figure set her apart from all others of her sex. This was a rare moment, as when one sees heaven in a flash of light, or an instant when one catches the rainbow's colours on the kingfisher's wing rounding the bend of a mountain brook, or when one glimpses the blood-red sunset locked amid the ochre clouds hanging over the dark-wooded horizon.

The Summer passed but the memory of that happy meeting at Llanwrtyd lingered on through the mist-laden days of September, when the drab, rain-laden loneliness of the Autumn pervaded the short days, and when long evenings were spent reading and chatting to Miss Parry, and my assistant, Miss Morgan. These were days when the full impact of my isolation made me wonder whether I should have accepted this post. My powerful motorcycle, however, offered a means of escape from my physical environment but alas, there was no fading of this visionary creature who haunted my thoughts day and night. I disclosed my intense dejection to Danny as I thought of some auspicious initiative that would provide the opportunity for another meeting with her. The daily fog and thick mist hanging over the bare woods and still countryside accentuated my misery and susceptibility to depression. My life lacked the vigour and liveliness of youth, while the impassivity and stagnation frustrated my impatient temperament. Every day replicated the day before, producing a tedium and dourness with more than a little cynicism and apathy at my repression.

Christmas, however, was celebrated in part at Llanwrtyd with one of the most prestigious events of the year in the Hunt Ball. Details of its grandeur were imparted to me by Danny when he spoke of the local élite, the aristocracy and the eminence of the local big wigs including, very importantly, the centre of my attraction. I was immediately electrified, eager, stimulated with the prospect of meeting and dancing with my enchantress. My brain bristled, my heart throbbed and as the days passed, I glowed with fervent enthusiasm and agitation.

Finally, the great day arrived and at tea-time, I paraded in my evening dress before the admiring gaze of Miss Parry and Miss Morgan. I could not contain my exhilaration and effervescence as I munched Miss Parry's rock cake. My thoughts were concentrated on the beautiful frocks, whirling to the Strauss waltzes, that were to be enjoyed after a sumptuous meal of grouse or duck, drunk with a vintage wine. I was so unused to the possibility of such upper-class celebrations that my mind wandered from the more arduous task of eating Miss Parry's rock cakes. Then disaster struck, my dreams were stifled as my jaws contorted in response to the cracking of my dentures! I left the table and examined what remained. It revealed the upper denture intact, but three front teeth in the lower plate had become detached although still attached to one another.

I wondered how I might effect some sort of repair, so that I could still proceed to the Hunt Ball which was due to begin in two hours. As a schoolboy I had read of a shepherd who had collected sheep's teeth to make a set of false teeth. He had wired them together. What could I use to re-attach these front teeth? My initial reaction was a death-wish followed by a convulsion of deep despair, but then a flash of inspiration - why not emulate that old shepherd and wire them up with thin electrical fuse wire? Success soon anaesthetized the source of my sadness as I wound the flexible wire, so that little of it appeared in front, as it was dextrously twisted and knotted on the inside of my denture. A little thumb pressure here and there made them a little more comfortable as they pressed on my gums. With my animation returned and my confidence restored, I donned my flying coat, goggles and helmet and sped into the cold darkness of the December night. The expectation of a wonderful dinner and ball cast out all feelings of coldness as the frosty air brushed against my face. My tongue slowly circumvented the prodding ends of the thin wire and, using my gloved forefinger, I pressed the offending end downwards.

My awareness of class difference came in the car-park, when the porter expressed some surprise at a guest parking a motorbike among the limousines.

"Excuse me," he said. "The car park is only for guests."

"I am a guest," I replied. "Here's my ticket," I added, much to his surprise.

He coughed, shook his head and disappeared into the foyer of the grand Lake Hotel, probably to complain of the decline since the Second World War of the standards of the middle-class. I was one of the nouveaux riches on a motor-bike!

I removed my flying coat, helmet and goggles before reaching the doors of the foyer. Inside local celebrities stood greeting one another as I passed into the cloakroom, trying my best to hide my gear. Few glanced in my direction as I moved in the medley of elegantly dressed ladies and well-fed, well-groomed gentlemen. I caught snippets of conversation such as,

"This is Commander ... and of course you known Brigadier ..., of course my dear, he is distantly related to Colonel .... of Llyswen."

Clipped accents, military moustaches, monocles and medals confirmed the presence of members of the landed gentry, many of whose ancestors had probably been Welsh-speaking chieftains and patrons of the bards.

I moved carefully and deferentially from the foyer into the smoke-room and dining area, now overflowing with groups of smiling, bedecked ladies in expensive frocks, drooping in gold necklaces and red-faced men joking, gesturing and drinking spirits. The refined tones emanating from the tall, trim statuesque figures expressing such esprit de corps, made me realize that I had no social or cultural identity among these gentlefolk. These were the descendants of the old County families who had for centuries provided the Lord Lieutenants, the Sheriffs and Members of Parliament for Breconshire. Even Crawshay, the millionaire iron-king of Merthyr, was excluded from their ranks because of supposed inferior breeding. These, after all, were the officer class of World War I, who had died in thousands in France and on the Dardanelles. My father was unsparing in honouring their bravery, but invariably added, "They had more to fight for than I did!"

I eventually spotted Danny and joined him when we were invited to sit at one of the round tables under the glimmering lights of the suspended candelabra. I sat opposite the young lady whose seductive enchantment had drawn me to this assemblage of shooting and hunting folk, people whom in fact I had been brought up to loathe, because of the class they represented and for the fact that they killed God's creatures for sport. Nevertheless, I was prepared to ignore these sentiments in the interests of overwhelming love of this snow-white-robed, raven-haired enchantress.

Eight guests sat around each table and immediately I caught the eye of the beautiful girl in white. For a second we were locked into each other's souls: it was again one of those ecstatic moments when God gives us a glimpse of heaven. It is that brief second when the rainbow is diffused on dark grey clouds, or when lightning flashes reveal the creator's glory in the skies. Her male companion followed her glance and, realizing danger, diverted her attention to the waitress and the pheasant, duck and other poultry heaped high on silver dishes. She smiled again and then the delectable meal was served, beginning with a superb soup and a main course.

As the guests piled their plates high with meat and vegetables, the conversation about dogs and horses was reduced to complimentary remarks about the various dishes. My eyes gravitated towards the meats and I eventually decided upon pheasant, which I had never tasted before, and because the cost of this function represented a fortnight's wages. I piled the plate with lump and layer of this deliciously fragrant meat. I dug the fork deeply into the inviting dish and leant back in my chair, savouring the most delectable food imaginable. I was ruminating on the fact that this was one of the most pleasurable experiences of my life, as I gazed around, chewed and tasted the exquisite flavour of well-cooked game. The fact that it had been hanging up for a fortnight and covered with maggots did not bother me one bit. I was even beginning to behave like the aristocracy. The meal was only beginning, and I looked at the laden table with eager anticipation. There was now a silence, with everyone voraciously watching the exquisite convoy of delicious delicacies arrive by the minute.

I adjusted happily to my situation, exchanging casual remarks on the quality of this repast with my neighbours, smiling at the beautiful girl opposite, while nonchalantly gazing at the sparkling chandeliers and the pink rose centrepiece in the ceiling. The waiters flitted from table to table, attending to the needs of the medley of retired officers, and a mixture of lovely, laughing ladies. They smiled in unalloyed delight at this opportunity for self-indulgence in food and drink. How different these were from the care-worn faces of the financially and socially deprived women of South Wales, living in valleys despoiled by industrialization and poverty!

While consciously and critically aware of the class difference between us in terms of status, wealth and power, I was nevertheless now confidently serene and thoroughly enjoying my expensive meal when, to my immense horror, I found that I could not swallow. I coughed, covered my mouth with my hand, and by dextrously probing with my tongue, realized that a large portion of meat was inextricably entwined in the wire supporting my dentures. I knew that if I could limit my conversation by averting their eyes, by pretence or by mute nodding, I might steal time enough to dislodge this glutinous mass and escape from this self-imposed torture. I fastidiously maintained a quiet decorum, while inwardly aware that I was totally ensnared, panicking and becoming dejected by this ordeal. How could I escape this nightmare?

The opportunity to use my fork as a lever came when all eyes and ears were directed to a long boring speech given by the red-faced, jolly Master of Fox Hounds. Unobtrusively, I manoeuvred the fork under the wire and was about to prise it further upwards when my dentures exploded and detonated like a bomb as the wire broke. My difficulties were now compounded by loose teeth, partly digested food and wire. There was no way to solve my problem other than to mumble some apology and slip away during the applause. Having disgorged and ejected the bulging entanglement into one of the flower-beds in the car-park, the feelings of disillusionment and magnified unease and distress were relieved by the balm of peace and darkness outside. The porter passed, "Leaving early, Sir? I hope you've enjoyed yourself."

"Yes, thoroughly," I replied as I smiled at the fact that I had been a hostage of circumstance, but had survived rather ingloriously my first night with the gentry.

Toilet Smashing and the 1947 Snow

THE SCHOOL AND OUTBUILDINGS, which included a small coal-house and toilets built by Miss Clara Thomas's family in the 1870s, bore no evidence of change. The three-section school with its walls of random stonework, roof of Welsh slate and green windows were well-proportioned and architecturally attractive. Inside, the painted walls were colourful and dry in spite of the very high rainfall. The uneven black oak floorboards, knotted and worn by decades of hob-nailed footwear, were a haven for both house and field mice, which occasionally peeped forth at quiet moments during the day. The toilets, however, presented a different picture. Because the white-washed brickwork had lost patches of its thick protective covering, its general appearance was one of neglect. It had no external doors to its male and female entrances, so that leaves and grass blew in with the rain and snow. A brick wall separated the boys' and girls' toilets, three on each end of the building. Each had a flaking painted door which scraped the earthen floors and opened into a closet of white- ribbed planks with a hole in the middle. Deposited behind a hinged flap in front was the toilet bucket. This was the standard toilet arrangement in the village and on the farms.

Mrs Evans of Cilderwen, my dedicated caretaker, was a widow living at the nearby Cilderwen Cottages and perhaps because her grandchildren, John and Betty Davies, were my pupils and used these toilets, she expressed more than a casual interest in the fact that there were wide vertical cracks appearing, indicating subsidence and a potential hazard. I well recall her drawing my attention to the danger: "Mr Bowen, this building is getting too dangerous to use."

"I will report it to the Education Office, Mrs Evans," I replied.

This conversation was repeated frequently during the following months when my stock reply was, "Mrs Evans, I'm tired of reporting the danger to the Education Office."

"They'll do something when someone is killed," was her usual reply. During the ensuing months my frustration was exacerbated by the formal acknowledgements to my reports, which were quite genuine. They were also based on the professional advice of my friends, Cyril Price, the village carpenter and undertaker, and Ralph Jones who also claimed some building expertise.

I had recently taught at Brynmawr Grammar School and at Vaynor and Penderyn Secondary School where the toilets were immaculate. Why should rural children have to endure the indignity of these primitive toilets? It didn't seem fair that this peasant culture outlook should persist any longer. I made up my mind in mid-October that something had to be done and very soon. I again examined the building, searching for the widest and most vulnerable cracks. I found what I was looking for. "That's the one," I thought, "Mrs Evans isn't going to be troubled much longer for her fifteen shillings a week in laboriously cleaning and scrubbing these daily." More importantly, the children would no longer endure the indignity and lack of privacy or the offensive odour in summer. The opportune moment would come probably before the end of the month. I worked on the details. Yes, it would be no problem on the right night.

In mid-October the weather changed suddenly when the beech trees at the bottom of the yard and the surrounding hedges became Autumn-dressed in a garland of golden browns and reds, and had their leaves savagely ripped away overnight. Storm-laden, dark scudding clouds and a wild westerly wind tugged and bent the trees. It increased in its destructive revelry, howling and lamenting in its relentless, powerful and rebellious mood, the lightning flashed and forked, splitting two-hundred-year-old oaks like matchsticks. Nightmarish, resonant thunder rolled through the bleak hills sending cowering animals to seek shelter. Throughout the sleepless night the heavens attacked the woods and fields, leaving behind in the silent dawn, bare broken-branched trees, swollen brooks, and the red soil pooled and sodden. The elements had taken revenge, retaliating for man's despoliation of the natural world. Broken slates, bent zinc sheets, lanes strewn with branches and dead leaves testified to the ferocity and tumult of the piratical wind and rain.

By nine o'clock most of the village children had arrived in school. The farm children came late, bedraggled by wind and rain, red-faced but smiling.

"Did you hear the wind last night?" asked David Smith. "Our shed has been blown over the hedge," chuckled John Davies as he removed his wet coat. Soon the guard around the tortoiseshell coal stove was steaming with piled garments and stockings.

Some farm children arrived around ten o'clock with cheerful sparkling eyes, cold hands and wet faces were rubbed and dried. Mrs Evans fussed from one stove to another with Miss Morgan, swapping coats for stockings to ensure that the clothes were aired for the return journey to the surrounding farmsteads. These were delightful, well-behaved children and upon reflection it was an honour to have been their schoolmaster.

The angry black skies presaged another night of storm and tempest. Leaves, tufts of grass and birds were thrown about the heavens, while the battered earth creatures crouched in terror against the bent bare hedges as the beeches groaned and cracked. A sudden forked flash of lightning over Epynt and the heavy rumble of thunder, followed by bangs of horrendous magnitude, rattled the windows and vibrated the very foundations of the school. Village parents arrived with coats and macs and umbrellas and Gerard's taxi soon carried Miss Morgan down to the village and the farm children to Abergwesyn and Llanafan Fawr.

This was the night I was waiting for. I explained my intentions to Mrs Evans and suggested that she should leave the premises as soon as it was dark in order for me to assist the wind and rain in the demise of the toilets!

"Good-evening, Mrs Evans," I called as she left at just after five as the rain lashed against the rattling windows.

"Good-night, Mr Bowen," she called. "Be careful."

"I'll be alright," I responded, hoping at the same time that my two chisels and heavy hammer would open the corner gap in the toilet wall, enough to bring the building down. However much noise I made, I felt it would not be heard against the roar of the screaming wind and the protest of the trees.

I allowed Mrs Evans ten minutes to leave the yard and reach the shelter of Cilderwen. How lucky I was that the tempest was raging outside; it would help me rid the school of the fungus-ridden, flaking white-washed walls, the dripping roof, the ribbed toilet seat planks and the miniature lakes of leaves and grass on the earthen floor. I blew out the Aladdin lamp, paused and listened, turned the 1870 key in the lock and walked into the wild black night. With my back to the torrent of rain, ducking the cascade from the asbestos roof, I felt for the crack in the brick-work. I pushed the chisel in and tapped it firmly into place, then with a resounding wham drove it into the gap. Nothing happened. I drove the other thicker wedge in and then the oak wedges one after the other. There was a slight movement. "This is it," I thought, "A few more taps and it will go but without any warning." I felt a shudder and stepped back just in time as the walls and roof crashed and cracked as the rotten roof-timbers snapped, sending the slates slithering in all directions. Lightning lit up the demolished building, now a pyramid, grotesque and silent.

With my collar up and my head bowed against the pouring rain, I leaned against the whirling wind as I wound my silent way over the carpet of sodden leaves. I left the school in darkness, with the ghosts of yesterday probably smiling at what the school-master had done! I felt both satisfied and justified. I thought of the owls who had nested and sheltered here over the years now wondering what had happened to their domain. They would have to rest in one of the many local barns, call from the sycamores around every farmstead, disturb the occupants and frighten the children. They would provide source material for the folklorists and their tales of the 'death bird', warning of impending funerals in the country churchyard at Eglwys Oen Duw!

The anger of the gales diminished during the night and the day began with silence, broken only by the swollen sounds of flood water almost touching the bridge over the Camarch. A cluster of children greeted me at the school gates with "Sir, the toilets have fallen down in the gale."

"Oh dear," I said, "what shall we do now?" Mrs Evans met me at the door, her face wrinkled in a smile and laughter in her eyes. "Sad about the toilets, Mr Bowen, we'll have to have new ones now, won't we?"

"Yes, it was a bad night, Mrs Evans," I replied.

"It looks as if it's been struck by lightning," chirped her grandson, John Davies.

"I think you're right, John," I replied as I hid my smile by walking into the school. We solved the problem of temporary toilets by using the school house toilets and in a month Ralph Jones, the local general factotum had built new ones that have weathered the storms and winter gales of the last fifty years.

In every village certain individuals stand out from the common herd by the charm of their personalities or special traits that mark them out as somebody rather special. Involved in the episode of the toilets were Mrs Evans and Ralph Jones, both of whom were very well-known characters beyond the confines of Beulah. Mrs Evans was so popular that when a meeting was called to organize a fête and choose a Festival Queen, it was unanimously decided that genial Mrs Evans should be honoured in this way. On the day of the crowning, Mrs Evans, gowned in a white satin dress covered by a Union Jack and a golden crown, was conveyed on to the Vicarage field on a superbly decorated gambo. The secret was well-kept and everyone was surprised, amused but pleased with the choice of this delightful lady as the carnival Queen.

Had I waited, the very heavy snow which fell the following January might have demolished the old toilets for me, thus saving me the trouble and anxiety. The older generation speak with some awe in referring to the snow of 1947 mainly because of its depth and the fact that it persisted from January until March. Hundreds of sheep died on the hills and mountain ponies were found standing dead in statuesque groups. Small animals such as rabbits struggled to survive, but were so weak that children at Beulah chased and caught them without difficulty. Even so, they were not worth eating because they were so thin. Obtaining food at Beulah became so difficult that supplies were only maintained by tractors bringing in supplies, and one weekend we were reduced to eating stale Swiss rolls.

The snow began on a Friday in early January and as I watched the first fleecy flakes whirl and cover the yard with a blanket of pearly whiteness, I decided that it would be advisable to dismiss the children early so that they could reach their distant homes before paths became obliterated, and before darkness descended over the bleak moorland and bare hilltops. They were duly warned to hurry home, not to deviate from the accustomed routes or loiter on the way.

Within the hour the fields and meadows had vanished under the shrouding snowflakes. Black hedges were beautifully transformed, each branch white-capped, while silhouetted trees stood gaunt against the bedded snow. Folded snow-cushions rounded the furrowed fields, filled the ditches, clung to posts and gates, draping and concealing the earth with whiteness. Birds fluttered from tree to tree in an alien world of total silence where hump-backed cows lowed loudly in protest at the unfamiliar scene of snow-gloved grass. Occasionally, the flurries stopped and the yellow sunbeams squinted through the leaden sheet of clouds onto the shimmering brilliance on the sheen of snow.

On Friday I drove my motorcycle carefully down the hill into the village, now numbed and silent with roofs, sills and gardens reposing under the quilt of white. I climbed the northern flank of Epynt, keeping away from the precipice on my left which dropped vertically into the shadows of Cwm Graig Ddu hundreds of feet below. Rabbits stood bewildered on the road in their first encounter with snow. Only when I was almost on them did they slowly hop into the safety of banked hedgerows, heavy with spiked icicles, clear as crystal. Above me a kite, fork-tailed, glided on the air currents searching for his evening meal before darkness crept over the moors. Mounds and hollows now filled in, except where some mountain stream forced its way through peat and rushes, stiff, proud but bending under the canopy of the newly fallen snow. Mountain ponies and sheep stood in forlorn, huddled groups, unmoving as if frozen to the earth.

Two hours later, having crossed the deserted gun-range on Epynt, I passed through Upper Chapel and Lower Chapel, where cottage lights glowed through curtained windows onto the wintry road leading to Brecon. Distant tolling bells in the towered cathedral beckoned the faithful to the evening service and the lamp at the lychgate revealed the winding outline of the path leading under the ancient yews to the open oak doors and the leaded Gothic windows, full of golden light pouring out onto the snow-bearded cedar trees and marble graves. The keenness of mullioned windows, the mouldings of doors and the outline of roof and tower were blunted now by the clinging snow. Black-coated figures trod an uneven pathway through the deep soft snow, greeted and waited to help each other on the steep hill climbing up from the town. The streets were ribbed with tracks leading to closed shops and open inns with doors momentarily ajar. The floor was a bed of potted and wrinkled frozen snow crunching loudly under the tyres of a few vehicles moving from the market. I recognized a car belonging to Mr Price, the butter merchant from Cefn Coed, and followed in his tracks out of Brecon and onto the Merthyr Road leading over the Brecon Beacons.

The car crawled and skidded in its upward climb along the winding road towards the Storey Arms. Here and there cars were abandoned with men and women, heads bowed against the driving snow, slithering on frozen patches and heading back to Libanus and safety. With legs outstretched, suffering agony when life in my feet was re-awakened by striking clumps of ice, I lost my guide and ploughed upwards and onwards through a foot of virgin snow, besieged in the most hostile environment imaginable.

By eight o'clock, and four hours after leaving Beulah, I was covered in a sheath of frozen snow, and welded to the tank with my hands bound firmly to the handlebars, until after much effort, I succeeded in freeing myself. As the blizzard developed, blanketing and drifting across the disappearing road, I realized that as I wiped my goggles and stared into the wilderness, where demons danced in flurries before me in the supernatural silence of these belligerent hills, I was facing death.

The higher I climbed towards the Storey Arms, the deeper became the snow barrier. Aching muscles, immovable feet, blinded by snow with icicles hanging from my nose and chin, I stopped somewhere near the Storey Arms, now barely visible in the swirling blizzard. I freed my hands from the gauntlets so firmly attached to the throttle and clutch and, leaning forward, tried to warm my hands on the engine. I cried as life was restored to my hands, and the instinct of self-preservation offered one opportunity for survival, and that was not to submit to my fatigue, but to drive forward through these murderous conditions suffering unremitting pain and discomfort, to find some sanctuary on the southern flanks of the Beacons.

I gasped in the frozen air; exhaled, it froze on my lips. I twisted, rose and fell as my bike bucked like an untamed horse in the mute drifts. I skidded downhill, recognized Crewe Pitch and, though exhausted, felt jubilant because I had somehow, miraculously crossed the most hostile, inhospitable tract of winter moorland in Wales. A dead horse in the middle of the road, abandoned cars, a lorry wedged across the bend of the road, an occasional shadowy figure struggling southwards towards Cefn Coed, relieved my terror of a lonely mountain death. Soon my father, waiting anxiously outside my home, guided me into our snug kitchen. He rained hammer blows on my chest to break the coat of armour enveloping my frozen body, and I cried again with pain as life was restored to my hands and feet. Over the years, I have drawn some comfort from the fact that I was the last to cross the Brecon Beacons for many weeks, when drifts of fifteen feet of snow blocked the roads until mid-March.

This was the worst period in living memory of sustained snowfalls lasting weeks, making whole areas isolated, roads impassable and causing destruction of flocks of sheep and mountain ponies. Even when sheep were brought down from the hills to the comparative safety of lowland fields, many either starved to death or were buried under drifts.

This horrendous winter was, however, followed by a lovely summer but even so, there were deep crevices on the Beacons still filled with snow in June. The government responded to this disaster by paying compensation to the farmers for lost stock. Because of an element of envy, I suppose, or of old feuds between neighbours and families, some farmers claimed that others had made fortunes by over-stating the number of lost sheep. Indeed, it would appear that some became more prosperous or retired early after that snowstorm of '47!

Deep snowfalls continued throughout February and school was closed for many days because of blocked roads. Scrawny rabbits struggled in the deep snow and sheep nibbled one others' tails and ate the bark off trees to survive. Getting adequate food supplies to the remote farms was very difficult. Men from Abergwesyn walked to Beulah, their backs covered with sacks pinned at the throat, and carrying essential food such as bread in sacks thrown over their shoulders.

Boredom and shortage of food prompted me to take some risks in an attempt to get home. A particularly heavy fall reduced the shops to only a rationed supply of Swiss rolls on one weekend. So on the Monday morning I decided to walk to Garth, some three miles away, where I hoped to catch a train to Builth Road, thence to Brecon and home to Cefn Coed.

It was a morning of high frowning clouds, the snow contrasting vividly with the black trees, telegraph poles and the distant brooding Epynt, white and dazzling in the morning sun. Snow slipped off the roofs, revealing here and there blue slates where birds pecked in vain for food. Cottage smoke ascended in swirling columns swept by the keen north wind that bustled through the cracking trees, and over the partially frozen river eddying between snow-covered boulders.

Dressed in the thickest clothes and wellingtons, I strode

through the deep- rutted carpet of white and was soon on the road, where drifts rose six feet over the hedges into the wayside meadows. Progress was exceedingly slow, the perverse snow hiding deep ditches and hedges where I sank up to my waist and chest. Finding the relative safety and ease of the road was difficult, but after two hours of trudging, sinking and struggling against the unyielding barricade of walled snow, I reached Garth Railway Station, two miles from Beulah. I emptied my wellingtons and for a few minutes eased my chafed and blistered feet. I waited for the train from Llanwrtyd, and after an hour my prayers were answered by the distant hoot and chug of the black engine, emitting puffs of steam into the frozen air.

I was the only traveller on the platform, and in a few moments boarded the train and was soon admiring the majestic grandeur of the snowbound hills, rising from wooded valleys with the dark grey Irfon full-flooded, foaming and gushing in black pools under overhanging crags. It was difficult to believe that this loveliness could bring fear and death in its grip. My thoughts came abruptly to a halt with the screech of brakes as we stopped at Builth Road Station. No assurance could be offered by the porter that a train would come to take me to Builth, so I decided to walk, This I found now to be quite an ordeal because walking in heavy rubber wellingtons over long distances is never easy, and by the time I reached Builth I was experiencing considerable pain in my frozen feet. I found a chemist and purchased bandages and a jar of Vaseline to relieve my agony. I found both socks soaked in blood due to broken blisters distributed over swelling toes and inflamed ankles. With my feet liberally plastered with Vaseline and swathed in bandages, I returned at about four o'clock to the railway station only to be informed that there were no trains to Merthyr because a train was stuck in the snow between Talyllyn and Torpantau.

My exodus from Builth was slow due to excruciating pain as I slipped, slithered and turned on the uneven lumps of ice and headed towards Builth Road still carrying my case of butter and eggs. Some two hours later, around seven o'clock, I found myself back at Garth and now confronted with the disheartening and long trek back to Beulah. It was a clear moonlight night with a full moon, clearly making visible the track that I should follow over the frozen snow, crunching and complaining under my feet. I frowned with frustration at my fruitless attempt to break out from my prison in the Irfon Valley. Floundering and fatigued, I was overjoyed to see the distant lights of the cottages at Beulah.

Accompanied by the screeching owls and the scent of wood fires carried in the night air, I at last opened the garden latch and the welcoming door of Glanyrafon. To be able to soak my blood-soaked feet in warm water, and to sit in front of Miss Parry's crackling fire, was a joy that can hardly be described.

By Friday, with my feet improved and the road to Builth cleared enough for single-line traffic, I again, with my butter and eggs, attempted to get home. Thankfully this time there were no problems at Builth where the train was on time in spite of the fact that large flakes were falling fast from the overcast sky. Only a few red-faced, heavily coated women and two black-suited men with bulging bags of groceries boarded the train. Although only six o'clock, the shadows of night were creeping over the hedged-in fields, and tree-covered slopes of hills descending to the black-ribboned Wye.

I changed trains at Talyllyn and found myself sitting with three women and two middle-aged men. The three women claimed they had been up to Brecon for various reasons, one to sell poultry in the market, another to do her shopping while the other, the wife of a Merthyr ironmonger, was up visiting relatives. Of the men one was known, so he claimed, as Johnny Pinafore, because he sold these garments in the markets of the locality, while the other was a Mr Vaughan who was a Merthyr solicitor, who had been prosecuting for the Ministry of Food in the Brecon Court that very day. The conversation was bright and cheerful, each traveller contributing some anecdote or information about the Black Market dealings, local prosecutions, their family successes or academic achievements.

"I've had a good day, anyway," laughed Johnny Pinafore, a

small, blue-eyed, pleasant bespectacled man who had left the pits to earn a living in the markets.

"Probably because the women were unable to do their shopping on account of the snow," suggested the lady who sold poultry.

"That's right," he said. "I've got my regular customers and I've not been able to come up for weeks. They were pleased to see me today because I always give them a fair deal."

"Been coming up for a long time, have you?" I asked.

"Yes, over thirty years. Mind you, it's not been much good because of the last war, but things were picking up until this snow came."

"Have you had a busy day?" I asked the solicitor.

"Yes," he replied. "I've been prosecuting for the Ministry of Food, mainly cases of people being caught with Black Market butter, bacon, meat or eggs." I sensed that everyone became a little ill at ease with this news.

"Were any gaoled?" I asked.

The women glanced at one another, one coughed with suppressed fear, another turned her gaze towards the window while the short plump lady who sold poultry said, "It's about time this nonsense came to an end. The war's over and still we've got rationing. What can you do with a few ounces of butter, margarine and sugar?"

"We must, however, abide by the law," said the solicitor. As he said this he was pitched forward onto the poultry dealer's chest as the train lurched to a halt. Johnny forgot his gout as he scrambled to the half-covered window.

"We're out in the heart of the country," he said. "I can't say where because the snow is pelting down."

"Well, we stopped at Talybont," said the ironmonger's wife. "So we're half- way between there and Dolygaer."

Johnny opened the window a little further and shouted, "Hey, guard, what's happening?"

"We're stuck in the snow."

"Good gracious, what will happen to us now?" asked the

poultry dealer as the guard, covered from head to foot in snow, pushed his head through the half-open window.

"We'll be here until they can come and dig us out. There was a train stuck here on Monday for 24 hours so try and keep yourselves warm." "I'm going to walk back to Talybont to let them know in Brecon that we're stuck here," he shouted as he disappeared into the darkness.

"We're here for the night, that's for sure," said Johnny, "and no food."

"I've got some butter," I said.

"And I've got two pounds of cheese," said the solicitor as he opened his briefcase, "but then it's no use without bread."

"I've got some B.U.s (bread units)," I replied "and I'll go back to Talybont to see if I can buy some bread."

I opened the carriage door and ran after the guard. We soon arrived at Talybont station and he hammered on the stationmaster's door. A bleary-eyed man poked his head around the door.

"It's me, Jim," said the guard. "We're stuck two miles up the track."

"You won't get any men out until morning," the Stationmaster replied.

"Come in anyway. Have a cup of tea."

With that his wife appeared and the situation was explained to her and I asked, "Do you think you could sell me a loaf of bread, please, I've got the B.U.s."

"Yes, certainly," she replied and within minutes I was making the return journey to the train. They were overjoyed when they saw the loaf of bread and knife which I had borrowed. The loaf was soon cut up, spread with butter and supplemented by pieces of American cheese so kindly provided by the solicitor.

It was a freezing night, hats were pulled over ears and faces were buried in upturned collars. We stamped out feet, pocketed our hands, blew on them, rubbed them and ate every morsel of bread and cheese.

We chuckled when Mr Vaughan said, "Mind you, I would never have bought this cheese. It was given to me by a friend."

"Can you get him to give you some more, Mr Vaughan?" asked Johnny. "I'll be glad to give you a little extra couple of bob if you can."

Mr Vaughan protested that this was outside the law but I noticed nevertheless a trace of amusement in the twinkle in his eyes. "We mustn't talk of these things in an emergency like this," he added.

"It's getting light," said the poultry seller. "Look at the snow, we've had about a foot in the night."

"We'll never get out from here," whimpered the ironmonger's wife. My husband's doing his nut over this," she added. "I wonder if he knows where we are?"

"They've got relief men coming from Brecon by now," said Mr Vaughan.

"Hugh, I can hear a train now," Johnny said.

"Yes, it's tooting to let us know we're safe," cried the ironmonger's wife.

"Thank God for that," said Johnny. "I thought it was all up on us and that we'd freeze to death."

Two hours later, I arrived at Cefn Coed and as I departed I heard Johnny shout, "Give your order for cheese to Mr Vaughan and we'll meet at the same time next week. Don't forget to bring the butter with you!"

"To Everything There is a Season." (Ecclesiastes)

WINTER TRANSFORMED BEULAH, IT revealed nature in a frightening mood. The joy of the springtime morning choruses, of the low red dawns, with the sky smoking red over verdant fields filled with spring life and strewn with meadow flowers were gone. Hedges run wild with green, were brittle with black trees. The gushing mountain streams have overnight become voiceless in the refrigerated air, whinnying and moaning through the woods. A mewing buzzard falls like a rock upon the white cushioned earth and a flapping raven sucks the eyes and tongue of a dying sheep. Timid creatures with bulging eyes scurry from the hovering kestrel, while the old and lonely shiver before peat fires in their isolated farmsteads, clinging to the black hills. Invariably, my journeys over Epynt were shrouded by the dragging mist. Apart from the throb of my motorcycle engine, I travelled in a silence broken only by the mist scurrying around the ghost filled habitations. Deserted farmsteads were crying for the once familiar sound of human voices and children's footprints in the morning dew. The red grouse rises from the heather, seeking his mate in the shadow of the deserted Drovers' Arms. Here a century ago, cattle drovers sought hot beer and warm beds on winter nights.

The ravished and exploited hills to the south of the Beacons, warned me on Friday nights, that I was approaching the "dark satanic mills" of my homeland at Cefn Coed and Merthyr Tydfil, once the iron kingdom of the world. Friday nights heralded my return to an industrial ravaged valley, emerging from the era of mass unemployment, a place of pale gaunt faced women and phlegm-spitting men, stooping and prematurely old. The women carried the scars of pre-war poverty, of dead babies and the memories of hundreds of boys killed in the two Great Wars. It was a community of lost leaders.

In contrast to my Friday evenings, filled with joy of warm companionship in the Cefn Coed library, my Sunday nights in winter presented the same kitchen scene. Chapel talk provided the themes for the conversation between my mother and aunt Marie. A mixture of my mother's nurses uniform and my motorcycling clothes, aired in front of the coal fire. The radio weather forecasts evoked considerable advice from my father, because snow or ice on the roads of the two highest mountain ranges in South Wales, were an obvious hazard. In my later years at Beulah, there was also developing a fear of accidents, as a result of a few skirmishes with death. These were always on the Epynt on my return journeys to Beulah.

My first real brush with death was a head-on collision with a lorry in the winter of 1949. This occurred near the mansion of Castell Madoc on a morning of heavy frost, sub-zero temperature and a biting wind which tore like a bush of thorns at my face. My breath froze and my lips and chin became firmly stuck to my great-coat collar. As I sped along the white winding road towards Pen-y-Fan, where 3000 feet of mountain was stabbing at the low clouds, I was blinded by swirling flakes of snow, mingled with rods of ice and sleet, covering me in a sheath of white armour. Without warning, I crashed on a river of thick ice, part of a castellated ice tower stepping up the snow laden mountain to my left. Slithering over the ice only caused me minor bruising and no damage to my motorcycle. After a respite, but now a little late, I continued on my journey through sleepy Brecon and then on the road towards Lower Chapel, Upper Chapel and the Epynt.

On the narrow road between Lower and Upper Chapel, I caught up with a slow moving council lorry carrying a number of workmen protected by a green canopy. I could not overtake the lorry and decided to wait, until I approached the straighter and wider road Castell Madoc. I opened the throttle and the 500cc engine responded with a roar as I came out to overtake the lorry, only to find another lorry speeding towards me! I recall trying to get up the bank on my right and then throwing myself off the motorcycle as we crashed into the front of the lorry. I found myself pinned to the ground with the lorry wheel on my shoulder. After some struggling I freed myself, stood up and found that the left leg of my trousers and my wellington had been torn off! My motorcycle was somewhere under the chassis of the lorry. I hobbled around to the lorry driver and of all things asked him, "have you got a light please?" There was no response, he merely sat motionless staring through the windscreen obviously in a state of shock.

By reversing the lorry the council workmen retrieved my motorcycle and my trouser leg and wellington! Somehow too, they replaced the motorcycle oil and straightened the bent kick starter.

In half an hour I arrived at school, having survived two mishaps on my journey. The lorry driver, however, was taken to hospital suffering from shock.

My second serious incident occurred again on the return journey to Beulah, only a few miles north of Castell Madoc. It was my custom on very cold mornings to stop near the red flag on the Epynt gun range. At eight o'clock in the morning the flag was always down, indicating that there were no guns firing on the range. Here was an ideal place to drink my morning coffee in peace and smoke a cigarette. Scattered over the hills were old farmsteads, once the homes of a community of farmers, who sought a precarious living from an unyielding soil and a harsh climate. Theirs was a perpetual struggle against poverty, pulmonary diseases, fears of the poor law, early death, damp houses and malnourishment. These were places with higher mortality rates than the urban industrial ghettos of Merthyr. Nevertheless, they somehow also survived the injustices imposed by the landed gentry, who owned their farms and the predatory foxes and hawks which attacked their stock. With their extremely limited financial resources they collected pennies to build little chapels in the valleys. They worshipped God with sweet voices and sad hymns, until they were ordered out of their homes to make way for a military gun range in 1939.

I visualised their journeys to the Christmas Plygain Services, the Harvest Festivals and the local Eisteddfodau. I imagined their sadness upon leaving farms that had been associated with their families for generations. Places where they had grown up, courted and married. They were leaving behind too, those hallowed plots where their loved ones were buried. But now it was time to move on, I finished my coffee, clipped my cigarette and then dropped the end into the pocket of my outer coat in which was a copy of J. B. Priestley's *"Good Companions."* I sped over the Epynt, crows flew out of the chimneys of the deserted Drovers' Arms, which for centuries had been a welcoming hostelry for the Welsh cattle drovers, en-route from Llandovery to English markets. Although the Inn is now used as a military store, gliding red kites and fluttering kestrels still grapple with the wind, while foxes, polecats and red grouse still mate in the halfpenny field at the rear. The field was so called because the inn keeper charged a halfpenny per cow per night for shelter.

I raced down the northern flank of the Epynt scattering dozens of rabbits into their wayside burrows. I was always acutely aware of Cwm Graig Ddu, a deep-sided valley, with its thousand feet drop over the black ledges of rock on my right. Soon the small hamlet of Garth appeared in the Irfon Valley. As I passed through the hamlet two roadmen dropped their tools, lifted the pokes of their caps and gazed at me in boggle-eyed amazement, as I passed by.

In a few minutes I arrived at Beulah and reduced speed to a crawl to round the bend in the village. As I did so, I felt a sudden surge of heat and found myself engulfed in flames. I stopped, ran across to the green roadside sward and rolled on the freezing earth to extinguish the searing flames. Whereas, a few moments before I was scorched by heat and fear, I was now uncontrollably shivering with cold. With the exception of the right arm of my flying coat, all my clothes had been burnt off and all my body was exposed to the elements. With no alternative, I remounted my motorcycle and drove up the road to school. Using some spare clothes and my ex-RAF trousers, I made myself warmer and respectable enough, to teach until 3.30pm, when I returned home to Cefn Coed, to replenish my stock of clothing and to pay the Cefn library for J. B. Priestley's book, *"Good Companions"* which had also vanished in the fire! I later met Mr. Morgan, Tŷ-Cornel, the roadman who told me that I was engulfed in flames, when I passed him and his companion at Garth. He also made me aware of the fact that the petrol tank on the motorcycle, could have exploded and that I was an extremely fortunate man to have survived this incident.

This experience made me fearful and anxious about my future at Beulah. I wondered whether I was doomed to endure many more winters of this agonising cold. I envied my contemporaries at Merthyr who taught in the local schools. On a salary of four pounds a week with the added difficulty of teaching thirty children between the ages of seven and fourteen years in the same room, was it worth all the hardship, danger and isolation?

After a weekend of pondering my future, I left Cefn Coed towards the end of January 1951, not realising that this was to be my last journey over the Beacons and Mynydd Epynt to Beulah. It had been snowing during the night and there was a thin covering over the road to Brecon. By the time I reached higher ground at Nant Ddu Lodge, there was about four inches of snow and ice. I avoided a dead piebald horse by the Nant Ddu church and halfway up the hill I realised that an articulated lorry was skidding backwards down the hill towards me. I turned just as the lorry jack-knifed across the road. I eventually got round the lorry and was able to warn the oncoming traffic of this danger lying across the road.

By the time I reached the Storey Arms, I had to drive with my feet dragging the ground because of the deep snow and the hidden underlying ice, where I had had an accident some weeks previously. Brecon was wreathed in white; I failed to proceed up the road by the Cathedral and had to find an alternative route through the side streets, to get on the Lower Chapel road to the Epynt range.

My motorcycle and my body became sheathed in a thick coat of ice and snow, with my nose and chin yet again, welded to my coat by ice. My hands, feet and legs were without feeling and my stomach shook with the intense cold. As usual on these cold mornings, I stopped to drink my hot coffee, but did not smoke again in this monastery of ice on the bleak Epynt.

The snow whirled in large flakes, drifts gathered on the road which was increasingly difficult to find. I knew that I was near the Drovers Arms; my speed was limited by the fact that my legs were spread-eagled in order to control my machine, which bucked like an untamed horse when we encountered deep drifts. I needed a continuous high level of concentration in order to avoid disaster in this wilderness of silence. Suddenly, I felt a body crashing against the side of the motorcycle with such force, that it was swept from under me. I hit the cushion of snow with the motorcycle on top of me and it was only with the greatest difficulty that I extricated myself. Lying dead and bleeding into the snow at my side was a massive ram. My body shuddered with shock and cold and I cried with the pain in my left leg. By the grace of God, exhausted and frozen and feeling ill I arrived at school two hours later. Only the village children were in school, all the farm children had wisely stayed at home.

During the day, I had frequent attacks of rigor when my teeth chattered and my knees knocked, as my body vibrated as if with fever. During the week, the pain in my leg worsened and I experienced difficulty in walking. Friday did not come too soon and when I returned home my mother examined my leg. She frowned when she measured my left leg and found it to be five inches bigger at the calf than the right. Dr Harold Thomas was sent for and he diagnosed that I was suffering from thrombophlebitis. I needed complete rest for several weeks with anti-coagulant drugs.

During my sojourn in bed the headship of Penderyn Primary School became vacant. I applied for this post and was shortlisted to appear for interview at the Brecon County Hall in a week's time. Against medical advice, I attended the interview, got the job and returned to bed for another month. I started as headmaster at Penderyn on April 10th 1951 and with regret, mixed with relief, left Beulah, convinced that, "to everything there is a season". It was time for me to leave.

Scotland Yard and Rural Characters

I FREQUENTLY TOOK MY CLASS past Dolaeron farm, through the woods to Dolaeron Woollen Factory, now closed, but occupied in those days by Mrs Williams, a widow with a son in Scotland Yard. She was naturally very proud of his achievements and during one of our frequent conversations I told her that I would like to meet him. My real intention was to ask him to visit the school and speak to the children.

The opportunity of meeting him came within a few days as I sauntered down the road from school one afternoon in late May. I recall that I was feasting my eyes on the newly green hedges, the greater and lesser celandines, primroses and dog-violets with their scattered gold and purple hues on the moss-strewn banks, and was reflecting on the fact that I had not found a bird's nest for years. Birds' nests had fascinated me from childhood when, in the company of Hugh Lewis, my cousin, I had roamed the hedgerows, woods and river banks at Cefn Coed in search of nests and in particular to find a nest with a cuckoo's egg in it. I recall vividly the excitement when Hugh found this rare treasure on the Navvies' Line in Cefn in the 1930s.

This memory was disturbed by the approach of a tall, broad-shouldered, smiling man, smartly dressed in a blue pinstripe suit with matching tie, carrying himself with a certain measure of confidence and assurance.

"You are Mr Bowen, I presume, since there aren't many strangers in these parts," he said.

"You are correct," I answered.

"My name is Detective Sergeant Berwyn Price of Scotland Yard," he said very proudly.

"Oh, you are Mrs Williams' son from the Woollen Mill," I replied.

"Yes," he said. "She's been telling me about you."

"I'm delighted to meet you, Sergeant Price. Where are you stationed now?" I asked, realizing immediately that this was rather a fortuitous question in view of the fact that he had said, "Detective Price of Scotland Yard." But rather to my surprise he said, "I'm stationed at Holyhead at the moment."

"Oh," I replied, "my former headmaster, Mr Trevor Lovett, is headmaster of the first Comprehensive School in this country and this is at Holyhead."

"The daughter of my landlady attends this school," he continued, "and Mr Lovett is a very highly respected headmaster and disciplinarian." I could vouch for both these qualities, having been a pupil and later teacher under him.

Nevertheless, hundreds of his former pupils would confirm his ability, integrity and dedication. In a recent broadcast on Radio Wales with Mr Vincent Kane, I quipped that an army recruit only had to state that he had been educated at Vaynor and Penderyn Grammar School under Trevor Lovett and he would be offered a commission in either the Airborne Division or the Commandos!

"Would you please convey my kindest regards to Mr Lovett, Sergeant Price, when you next see him?" I asked.

"Certainly," he said and we walked in our different directions.

"Goodbye, call in at the school when you have a few minutes to spare," I shouted. "I'll do that, thank you," he said. "I'll be delighted to revisit my old school."

My thoughts turned back to my glorious days at Vaynor and Penderyn with its aura of industry and scholarship, dedicated teachers, the grandeur of the school plays and the intense significance of the Speech Days with some of the most eminent scholars and celebrities of Wales as guest speakers. One can imagine the abiding impression made on the pupils and the sacrifices made by parents to keep their children in school, when the total income for most of the families was limited by dole and the dreaded Means Test, which, for example, allowed a man, wife and two children one pound six shillings a week to live on. Trevor Lovett understood all this, and he felt it his duty to drive his pupils and staff mercilessly to attain excellent results. It was no accident that three pupils in one form became professors of medicine, another a professor of chemistry, another the first Fellow of Harwell and a girl who became a Reader in Cambridge.

Although I had kept up correspondence with Trevor Lovett after his move to Holyhead I had not seen him for a few years. It was therefore a great pleasure to meet him with Mr Morris, a noted H.M.I., in the foyer of the Metropole Hotel at Llandrindod, when I arrived with Mr Gwyn Williams, Deputy Head of Ysgol y Graig, to attend a week's course the following June after meeting the detective. Much to my surprise, I found his demeanour rather frosty. He turned to Mr Morris and introduced my colleague, "This is Mr Williams of Cefn Coed and this is Bowen, a former pupil, and member of my staff at Cefn. Furthermore, if I had seen him a fortnight ago I would have given him the finest kick in his a... that he's ever had."

"Why, Mr Lovett?" I asked in surprise.

Without answering he turned to Mr Morris and said, "You were in our Speech Day at the Town Hall, weren't you?"

"Yes," replied Mr Morris.

"Do you recall that most embarrassing moment for me during the interval when, in front of all the guests and Governors, I was hailed by that Detective Sergeant from Scotland Yard who shouted 'Are you Mr Trevor Lovett?' "

"I nodded my head and said 'Yes,' and then this policeman said, 'I'm Detective Sergeant Price of Scotland Yard, could I have a word with you outside please?' "

"I recall that very well," said Morris. "Everyone thought that you'd been arrested."

"Do you know," said Lovett, "I was so shocked that I could hardly follow him outside, because I too thought that I was being arrested."

"I can assure you," said Morris, "that everyone thought likewise."

"Well, when we got outside," said Lovett, "this Detective said to me, 'Elwyn Bowen sends his kindest regards'." My reply was brief, " 'To hell with Elwyn Bowen,' I said."

"When you returned and told us this story we were all very relieved," said Morris, "and we all saw the funny side of it."

"I didn't think it was funny then," said Lovett, "but I do now. Nevertheless, let me repeat - you would have had the finest kick up your a... that you'd ever had in your life I can assure you," he said with a smile and a handshake.

Sergeant Berwyn Price of Scotland Yard had certainly frightened Trevor Lovett, a man who had been a fighter pilot in the First War, and gave the appearance afterwards, as the headmaster of the Grammar School at Cefn Coed, of not being afraid of anyone. I chuckled as I thought of this man suffering the trauma of intense fear, such as I and many others had experienced outside his study door at Cefn. Berwyn, apparently, was a local charismatic character who was capable of making the most of such an occasion. It was amusing, and I suppose quite ironic, that a character from a remote rural village should have reduced the great man almost to tears. I was soon to meet many other fascinating rural characters, one actually the day following my return to Beulah upon the completion of the course at Llandrindod.

It was V.E. Day, the 8 May 1945, when the war in Europe ended at 3.00 pm and Victory in Europe was being celebrated as a public holiday, that I met Ralph Jones for the first time. As I approached the bridge over the Camarch I could see a uniformed soldier of around forty years of age with sparkling blue eyes, standing on the bridge facing me, his face wreathed in a broad smile.

"Hello," he said, "are you Mr Bowen?" I confirmed that I was and he then introduced himself, "I'm Michael and Dennis Jones' father." We shook hands; there was an immediate empathy between us and a long lasting friendship was launched there and then.

"Are you coming over to Llangamarch tonight?" he asked and before I could answer said, "They've organized a V.E. dance there, come with us."

I agreed to go. "Right, what time?" I asked.

"Seven o'clock at my house. I live in the last house on the right hand side," he said with a smile.

After tea with Miss Parry, with her face radiating warmth and happiness at the declaration of peace in Europe, I set forth to join Ralph and learn something of the locality. When I arrived at his home I was introduced to his wife, while the two boys were smiling from their respective corners near the fireplace.

"How are we getting there?" I asked.

"Well," said Ralph, "we'll walk down the road to where the back road to Llangamarch meets this road, then I'll ride about a mile on the bike while you run. When you find the bike on the roadside, you will then ride until you pass me and after about a mile leave the bike on the side of the road and I'll pick it up. We carry on like this until we reach Llangamarch."

Ralph offered me the first ride but out of respect for his ownership of the old bike and his age I said, "You go first and I'll follow." The large twenty-eight-inch-frame bicycle meant that the short plump figure had to bend from side to side to reach the pedals. However, away he went into the dusty silence of the wending white road. I puffed along the narrow road which opened onto Caerau farm and the Roman fort on the left and Llwyn Cadwgan on my right. My pounding feet disturbed three cuckoos on the telephone wires which, with their two-fold calls, no doubt worried the finches and linnets and other meadow and hedgerow birds nearby. Sky-whirling and crying were hundreds of curlews, swooping in to land and run quickly to their unprotected nests on the ground. Gliding gracefully above were the red fork-tailed kites watching with fierce, black-spotted eyes the antics of a stoat following a crying terrified bunny calling for its mother, and sheltering herself from prying eyes, and the vice-grip talons of the silent marauding shadow above.

I found the old bike lying in the bullrushes and in a few minutes passed a very red-faced soldier, blowing and sweating while bending down to touch his toes, and shouting some encouragement to me. In a short time, after a few rides and runs, I rode down a steep winding road, past a majestic towered church with a large white-washed farm on my right. I was now very near to Llangamarch with its blue Welsh-slated roofs and white-washed walls.

I had never heard of this form of transport before but it got us to Llangamarch in a very short time. My first impression of this spa village was of a wayside hotel near a railway bridge, a village square with one or two shops, a saddler's shop and a long street of cottages on each side of the road going northwards. On the right side of the road was the village hall, a grey-painted, zinc-sheeted building, rectangular in shape with a small porch adjoining the pavement. Outside, stood a number of men talking and teasing the ladies passing to and fro, with dainty cloth-covered trays laden with cakes. They in turn made jocular remarks, causing the red-cheeked farmboys to burst into loud laughter, as they in turn added some funny remarks about route marches between the currants in the cakes, of breaking teeth on the Welsh cakes or of peptic ulcers from the goldfish sandwiches.

I waited for ten minutes for Ralph to arrive. "Follow me," he gasped and led me into the village hall. He was obviously an exceedingly popular and well-known character, because from every quarter came greetings and "Hello, Ralph" seemed to be on everyone's lips. He introduced me to what must have been the total population of Llangamarch, squashed like sardines into the hall to celebrate this very important occasion. There were farmboys smelling of carbolic soap dancing with thick-legged girls with tweed skirts and black heavy shoes. Older ladies, smiling through false teeth and spectacles, did their best to encourage everyone to eat the thick slices of currant cake, sandwiches of fresh bread, lined with egg or tinned salmon and tomatoes. The men munched, laughed and nearly choked as they made the most of this free fare, calling at the same time to the budding Fred Astaires on the dance floor, who had discarded nailed boots for their Sunday-best black boots. Girls, grouped in corners, squinted and evaluated potential spouses among the moving mass of shuffling feet, vainly attempting to move in unison with Tommy Edwards on the drums, and his pal banging the three-legged, worm-eaten piano, which pleaded through discordant notes for the first tuning after fifty odd years of thumping by aspiring local pianists. I struggled on the knotted dance-floor with girls and women more accustomed to the robust activities of farm life than attempting to follow Tommy's ill-timed efforts to keep us moving.

This was my first taste of rural leisure-time activities and over the years Ralph and I attended the Pancake Day whist-drive and dances at Llangamarch, costing one shilling and sixpence and also the Christmas whist-drives at Garth, Llanafan, Llanwrtyd and Llangamarch. In the six and a half years that I spent at Beulah I can never recall Ralph ever failing to win the first prize of a fat turkey or goose at the local whist-drives. Getting the turkey back to Beulah presented some difficulty in view of the form of transport that we were employing. The one doing the running stint had to carry the poultry. We could not leave it with the bicycle, because the area was an ideal habitat for foxes, stoats, weasels and polecats. It was not easy running with a fourteen-pound turkey under your arm!

As a result of a frightful accident to Ralph in the Autumn of 1950 these forages into the local villages came to an abrupt end. Ralph was perched on the top of a gambo receiving pitchforks of hay in one of the Llwyn Cadwgan sideland fields, when the load toppled sideways, throwing Ralph onto a pitchfork which was standing upright, with the handle stuck in the ground. The fork passed through Ralph's chest, protruding from his back and through his left arm. He fell sideways, and when he stood up the fork handle lay horizontally in front of him, Bill Knott, the farmer, rushed him by lorry to Builth Cottage Hospital, where he lay critically ill for some time. He was discharged from hospital at Christmas, now an invalid and with a form of creeping paralysis starting in his legs, which gradually made him a paraplegic.

After my accident by the Drovers' Arms on Mynydd Epynt in January 1951, when I collided with a sheep about 8.30 am in a blinding snowstorm, I suffered a thrombosis in my leg which kept me bedridden for weeks. During this time I was appointed Headteacher at Penderyn and left Beulah at Easter 1951. During the following May I was informed by the County Auditor that Ralph was now very seriously ill. On the following Saturday, fully recovered from my own illness, I left Cefn Coed and arrived at Beulah at midday. I enquired of Mrs Evans at the Post Office about Ralph and she told me to enter Ralph's house where I would find him in bed in the front room.

I walked towards his house thinking of those many happy occasions when we had enjoyed playing draughts in Elvet Powell's farm at Maesllech, and attending whist- drives and rural dances together. I opened his front door, walked along the passage calling out, "Hello, Ralph," and entered his parlour to find him lying in a single bed by the fire. He was unable to speak to me, his voice and ringing laughter now fallen silent. Using his eyes as a means of communication he directed my gaze towards the mantleshelf on which was a box of matches, a packet of cigarettes and a writing pad and pencil. Thinking that he wanted a cigarette, I lit one but he refused it. Without being able to look at the writing pad and only barely able to clutch the pencil, he scratched the word 'salmon.' I looked at him as the tears rolled down the side of his face onto the white pillow. Tears filled my eyes too, as in that total vacuum of sound, our minds were brimful of exciting and meaningful memories, spent under the stars on riverbanks near Beulah. A few days later I heard he had passed away and so ended a sincere friendship with a true countryman and lovely personality.

My six years at Beulah introduced me to a new and different culture. Here I found a close community of hard-working, reserved, generous people whose roots were in the soil and tied by cross-cutting ties of family, religion, language and custom. I witnessed a society changing from a self-sufficient community into one depending upon outside agencies for its food, clothes, shoes, tools and equipment. Within a year of my leaving in 1951 the wheelwright's shop, worked for decades by Dai Arthur, and the blacksmith's shop, worked by Jim Mathias, were closed for ever. Horses were being replaced by tractors and cars. I was honoured and privileged to have been part of this community as headmaster of Llwyn Madoc School from 1945 to 1951. The school is now closed, and the pupils travel daily to a new school in the neighbouring village of Garth.

TREGARON
Llanddewi
Brevi
Olmarch
Bettws
Llanbadarn
Capel Bettws
Blaenpenal Chapel
Llangeitho
Aberarth
Aberayron
Cilcennin
Nantgunllo
Abermenick
Llanlio
King Mead
Ystrad
Dyhewyd
LAMPETER
Pencarreg
Llanybydder
Llanwenog
Teivi River
Kellan
Llanycrwys
Llampeter
Cynwil Gaio
Dole Cothi
Mines
Pymsaint
Forest
Capel Filin
Ystrad Fin
Cwm Berwin
Dol Goch
Dublin
Glanbran
Henllys
Llwyn Howell Hall
Llansawel
Llansadwrn
Talliaris Park
Talley
Abergorlech
Edwins Ford
Cothi River
Llanllawddog
Llangwilli
Llanllawddog
Gwirgrig
Plas bach
Newlan
Llanvihangel Rhosycorn
Abermarles
Cross y Ceilon
Maesydin Inn
Myddyai
LLANGADOG
Pontarllechau
New Houses
Towey River
Mynydd Trecheg
Manarvabon
LLANDEILO VAWR
Caer Cennin Castle
Cennen River
Capel Gwynvai
Black Mountain
Llanvihangel Kilyargen
Llanarthney
Aberbervthig
Llangunnor
Llandybie
Dyffryn
Cross Inn
Bettws
Capel Llaningwithon
White Hall
Pontar Hydd
Braudey
Llangyndeyrn
Colebrooke
Pentybeyron
Llaned
Llan Non
Tylo
Parkeam
Llangunwg
Pentre Castle
Kilybebill
Cadoxton
Capel Dyddgen
Llangennech
Pontar Dulas
Dulas River
Llandeilo Talybont
Llougher River
Llanelly
Pinget
Penbree
Kidwelly Marsh
Capel Dewis
Llougher
Llansamlet
Cadley
Rhy y Pandy
Pont ar Glasen
Capel Lago